I CAN MAKE IT! I CAN READ IT!

Grade 1

20 Reproducible Booklets to Develop Early Math & Literacy Skills

Managing Editor: Deborah G. Swider
Contributing Writers: Ada Goren, Lucia Kemp Henry, Angie Kutzer, Suzanne Moore
Copy Editors: Sylvan Allen, Karen Brewer Grossman, Karen L. Huffman, Amy Kirtley-Hill, Debbie Shoffner
Cover Artist: Nick Greenwood
Art Coordinator: Cathy Spangler Bruce
Artist: Cathy Spangler Bruce
Contributing Artist: Lucia Kemp Henry
Typesetters: Lynette Dickerson, Mark Rainey

President, The Mailbox Book Company™: Joseph C. Bucci
Director of Book Planning and Development: Chris Poindexter
Book Development Managers: Elizabeth H. Lindsay, Thad McLaurin, Susan Walker
Curriculum Director: Karen P. Shelton
Traffic Manager: Lisa K. Pitts
Librarian: Dorothy C. McKinney
Editorial and Freelance Management: Karen A. Brudnak
Editorial Training: Irving P. Crump
Editorial Assistants: Terrie Head, Hope Rodgers, Jan E. Witcher

www.themailbox.com

©2002 by THE EDUCATION CENTER, INC.
All rights reserved.
ISBN# 1-56234-509-5

Except as provided for herein, no part of this publication may be reproduced or transmitted in any form or by any means, electronic or mechanical, including photocopying, recording, or storing in any information storage and retrieval system or electronic online bulletin board, without written permission from The Education Center, Inc. Permission is given to the original purchaser to reproduce patterns and reproducibles for individual classroom use only and not for resale or distribution. Reproduction for an entire school or school system is prohibited. Please direct written inquiries to The Education Center, Inc., P.O. Box 9753, Greensboro, NC 27429-0753. The Education Center®, *The Mailbox*®, the mailbox/post/grass logo, and The Mailbox Book Company™ are trademarks of The Education Center, Inc., and may be the subject of one or more federal trademark registrations. All other brand or product names are trademarks or registered trademarks of their respective companies.

Manufactured in the United States
10 9 8 7 6 5 4 3 2 1

TABLE OF CONTENTS

Acorns for Sammy (Writing Numbers to 100) 3

Busy Bee's Birthday (Comparing Whole Numbers) 8

Even Steven (Fractional Parts of a Whole) 13

Fishy Fractions (Fractional Parts of a Set) 17

Home, "Tweet" Home (Using the Associative Property of Addition) 21

Parrots, Monkeys, and Ants, Oh My! (Skip-Counting) 25

Delightful Dragonflies (Writing Number Sentences to Solve Word Problems) 29

Pets Galore (Identifying Attributes) 34

Kanga Makes a Pattern (Patterning) 39

Shep's Shapes (Identifying Plane Figures) 44

Frog's Busy Day (Relative Positions) 49

Sally's Shapes (Identifying Solid Figures) 54

Beaver Builds a House (Identifying Plane Figures) 59

Worm Wakes Up (Measuring in Inches) 63

"A-weigh" We Go! (Comparing Weights) 67

Ticktock! (Telling Time to the Hour and Half Hour) 72

A Home for Goldie (Capacity) 77

Which Mouse Measures Up? (Comparing Lengths) 82

Graphing Garden Goodies (Collecting, Graphing, and Interpreting Data) 87

How Many Animals Are in the Zoo? (Reading a Picture Graph) 92

ACORNS FOR SAMMY

Sammy seems to have forgotten something. Use this interactive booklet to reinforce writing numbers to 100 and to help Sammy find out how many acorns he has buried. Give each student a copy of pages 4–7. Read the booklet pages with students. Then instruct each student to color her cover and booklet pages and cut them out along the bold lines. (Remind students not to color the acorns so they can write on them.) Show students how to glue the pages as indicated. Next, instruct each student to use the numbers shown as clues to help her write the missing numbers on the acorns. Then have the student accordion-fold her pages as shown. Invite each student to read her completed booklet with a partner before taking it home to share with her family. Everyone will be nuts about it!

CREATIVE DECORATING OPTIONS

- Paint the sky on each page with blue watercolor.
- Glue cotton balls on for clouds.
- Decorate the tree with pieces of real fall leaves.

As a literature extension, read aloud *Squirrels* by Brian Wildsmith. Then invite students to draw a picture of something new they have learned about these furry friends.

Booklet Pages

BUSY BEE'S BIRTHDAY

Get your students buzzing about comparing whole numbers with this interactive booklet! Give each student a brad, a 5" x 7" piece of colorful wrapping paper, and a tagboard copy of page 9 and the wheel on page 10. Provide him with a copy of the booklet page on page 10 and a copy of pages 11 and 12. Read the booklet pages with students. Then instruct each student to color the Busy Bee pattern and the booklet pages. (Remind students to color lightly over the text so the booklet can be read.) Next, have the student cut out his booklet pages and tagboard wheel along the bold lines. Show the student how to cut along the dotted lines on each page and the Busy Bee pattern to make windows. Help him insert the brad through the center holes, first through the Busy Bee pattern and then through the wheel. Next, tell the student to trace a booklet page onto the wrapping paper and then cut out the tracing. Have each youngster stack his pages in numerical order, place the wrapping paper page on top, and staple the booklet along the left-hand side. On each page, direct the student to count the bugs and then write the corresponding numbers in the blanks. Have him spin the wheel to display the *greater than, less than,* or *equal to* symbol that correctly compares the two numbers. Instruct the student to read the complete number sentence quietly to himself. Encourage students to practice reading their booklets with buddies before taking them home to read to their families. So, that's what the buzz is all about—number sense!

CREATIVE DECORATING OPTIONS

- Glue a triangle of colorful wrapping paper and a few crinkled pieces of tissue paper to Busy Bee's party hat.
- Attach a miniature bow to the center of the wrapping paper page.

Extend this booklet by inviting students to create their own number comparisons with bug-design rubber stamps. Have each student stamp a desired number of bugs on the left-hand side of a sheet of paper. Next, have him do the same with a different bug design on the right-hand side. Then tell the student to write the corresponding number below each set of bugs and the correct symbol (>, <, or =) in the middle.

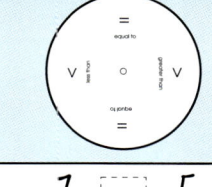

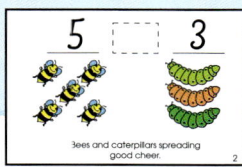

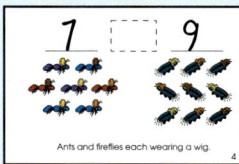

Booklet Backing Page

Busy Bee's Birthday

Buzz! Buzz!

> greater than   ○   < less than

= equal to

Staple booklet pages and cover here.

©The Education Center, Inc. • I Can Make It! I Can Read It! • Math • TEC3520

Note to the teacher: Use with "Busy Bee's Birthday" on page 8.

Wheel Pattern and Booklet Page

Wheel

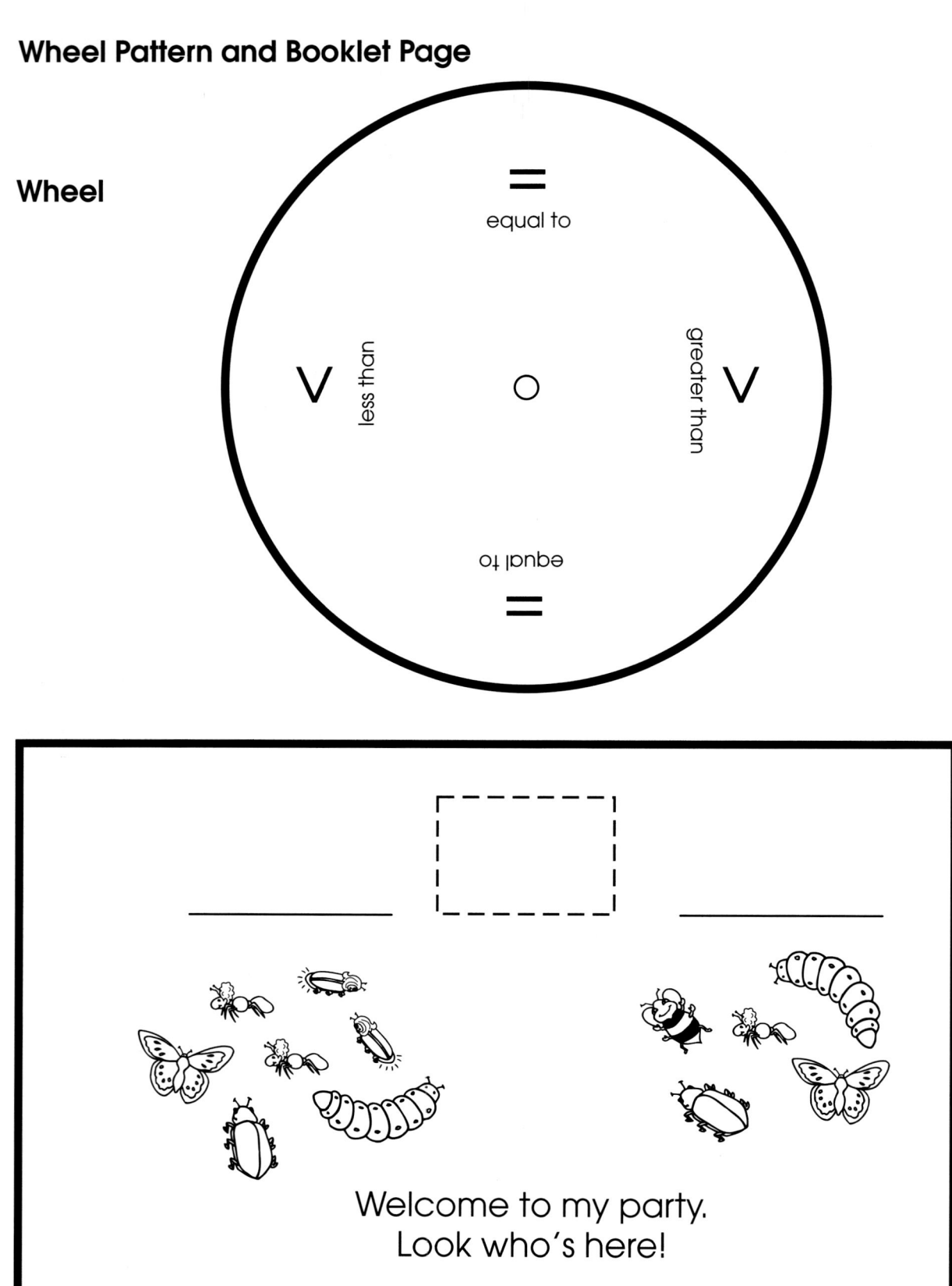

Welcome to my party.
Look who's here!

1

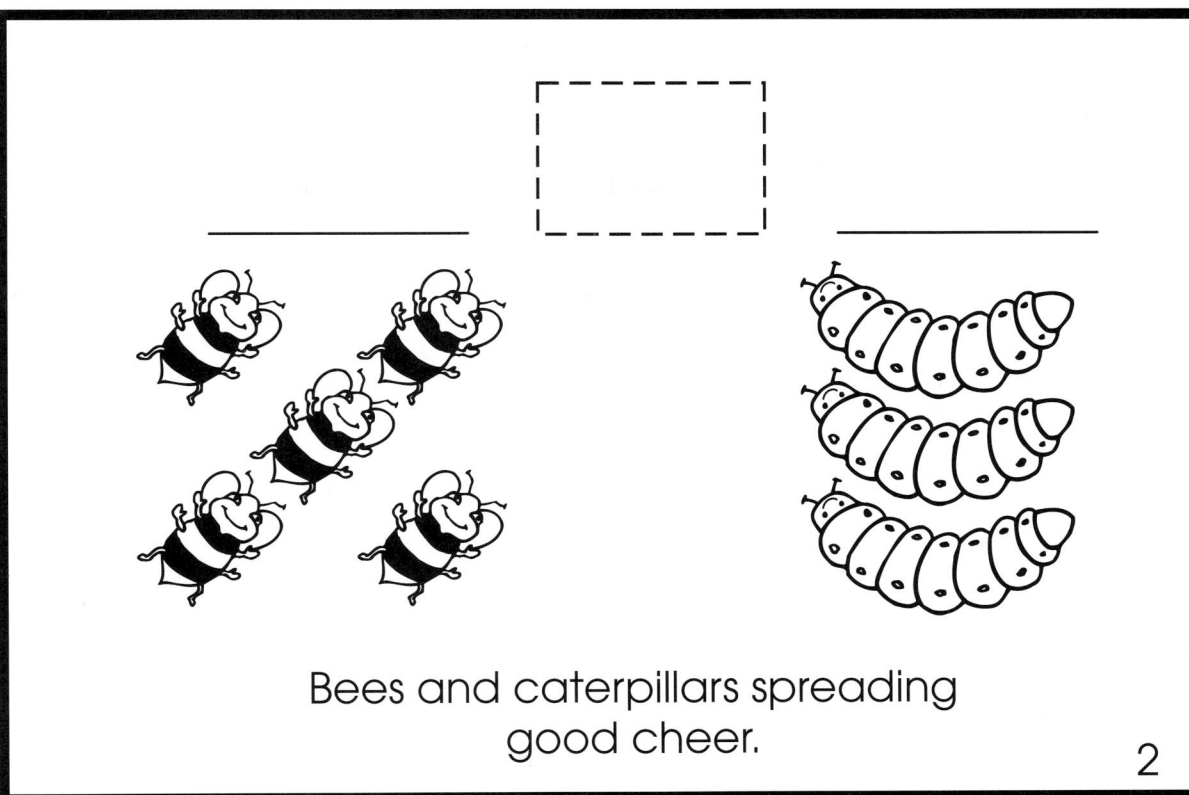

Bees and caterpillars spreading good cheer.

2

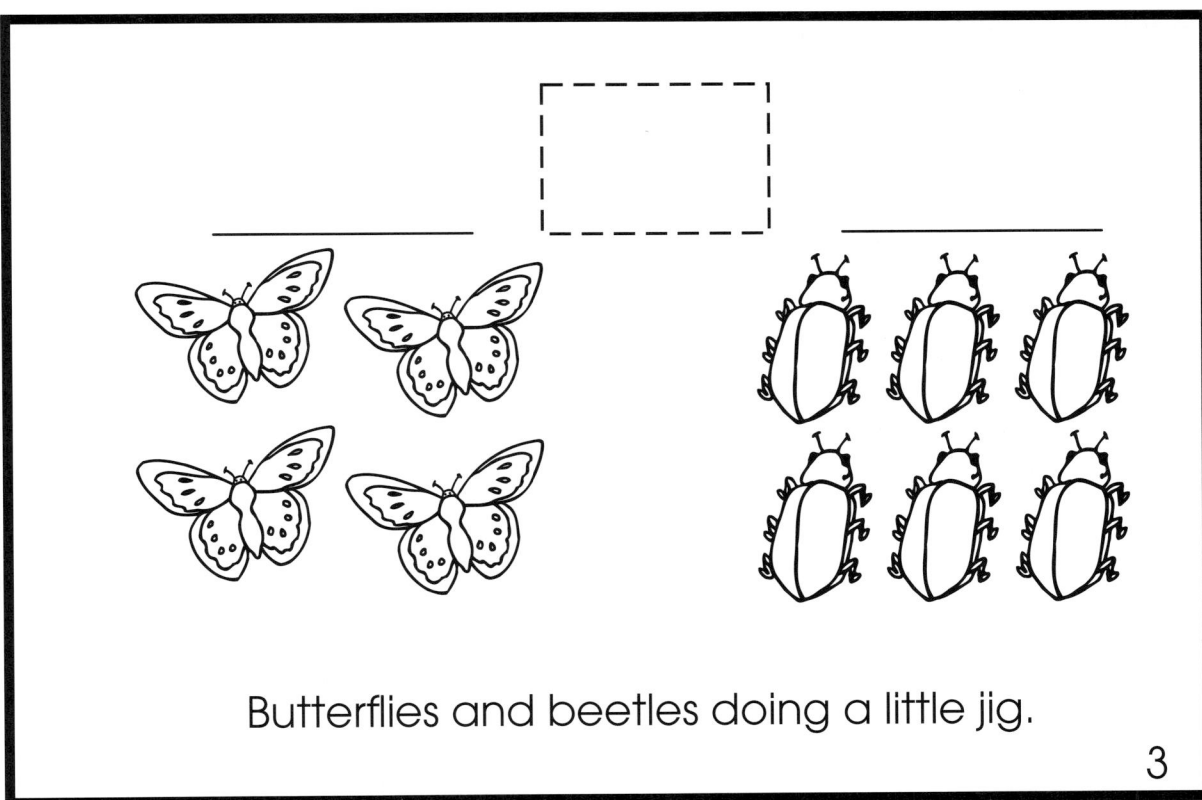

Butterflies and beetles doing a little jig.

3

Booklet Pages

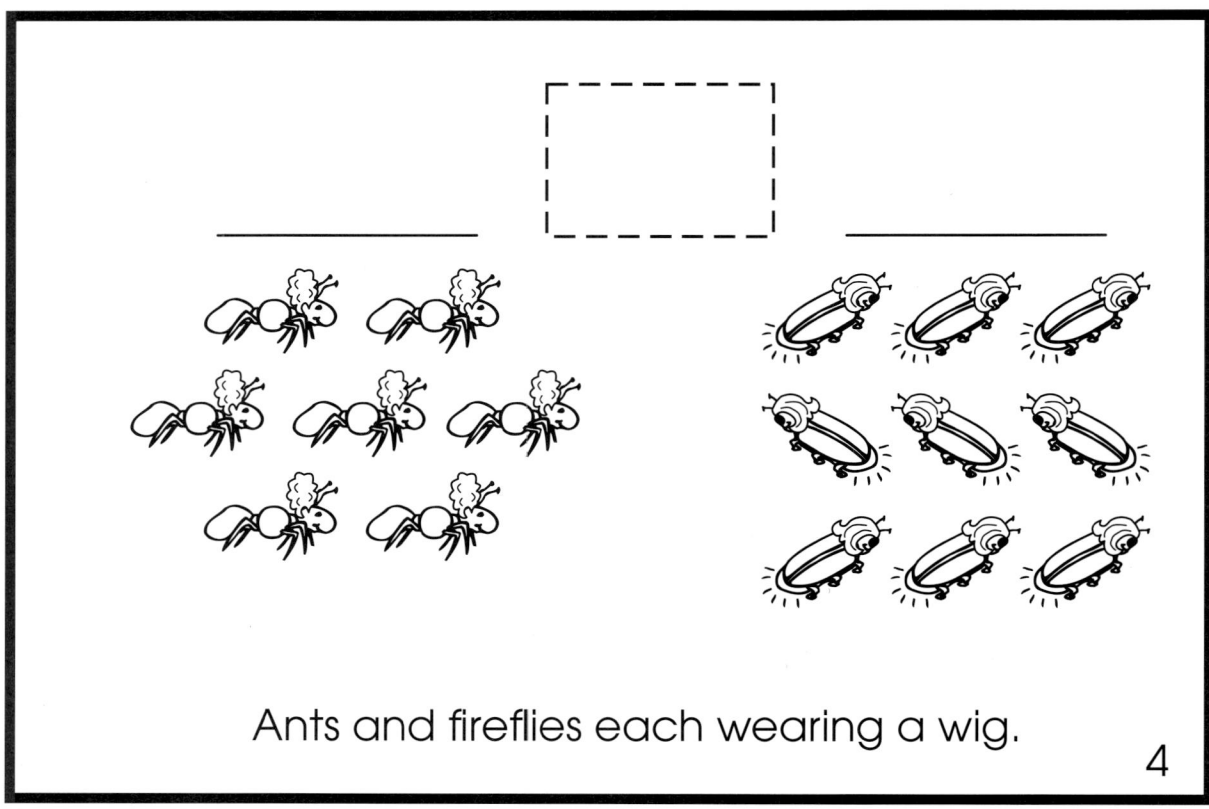

Ants and fireflies each wearing a wig.

4

Wow! Busy Bee's party is getting very big.

5

©The Education Center, Inc. • *I Can Make It! I Can Read It!* • Math • TEC3520

EVEN STEVEN

Teaching fractions as part of a whole is s-s-simply s-s-super with this fun booklet! Give each student a copy of pages 14–16. Have each student color and cut out the cover. Then instruct her to cut out the booklet pages along the bold lines. Next, read the text on each page together. Have each student draw the corresponding number of lines to evenly divide Steven's body as directed on each page. Have the student color the snake according to the text and then color the rest of the page. Tell each student to stack her pages in numerical order with the cover on top. Help the student staple her booklet along the left-hand side. Invite each student to read her completed booklet with a partner before taking it home to share with her family. What a "fantas-s-stic" review of fractions!

CREATIVE DECORATING OPTIONS

- Glue wiggle eyes on Steven's face.
- Glue on a short length of red ribbon or yarn for a tongue.
- To make the booklet reusable, staple a piece of laminating film over Steven's body on booklet pages 2–5. Have a child use dry-erase markers to color Steven as directed on each page. Then wipe the film clean with a baby wipe or damp cloth to start again.

To extend this booklet, give each child a few Gummy Worm candies and a plastic knife. Ask her to divide each worm into halves, thirds, or fourths. Then allow students to enjoy eating their newly created fractions.

Booklet Cover and Page

Even Steven

by _____
Name

Staple.

This is Steven the Snake and his friend Max. Max is an artist.

©The Education Center, Inc. • *I Can Make It! I Can Read It!* • Math • TEC3520

Note to the teacher: Use with "Even Steven" on page 13.

Booklet Pages

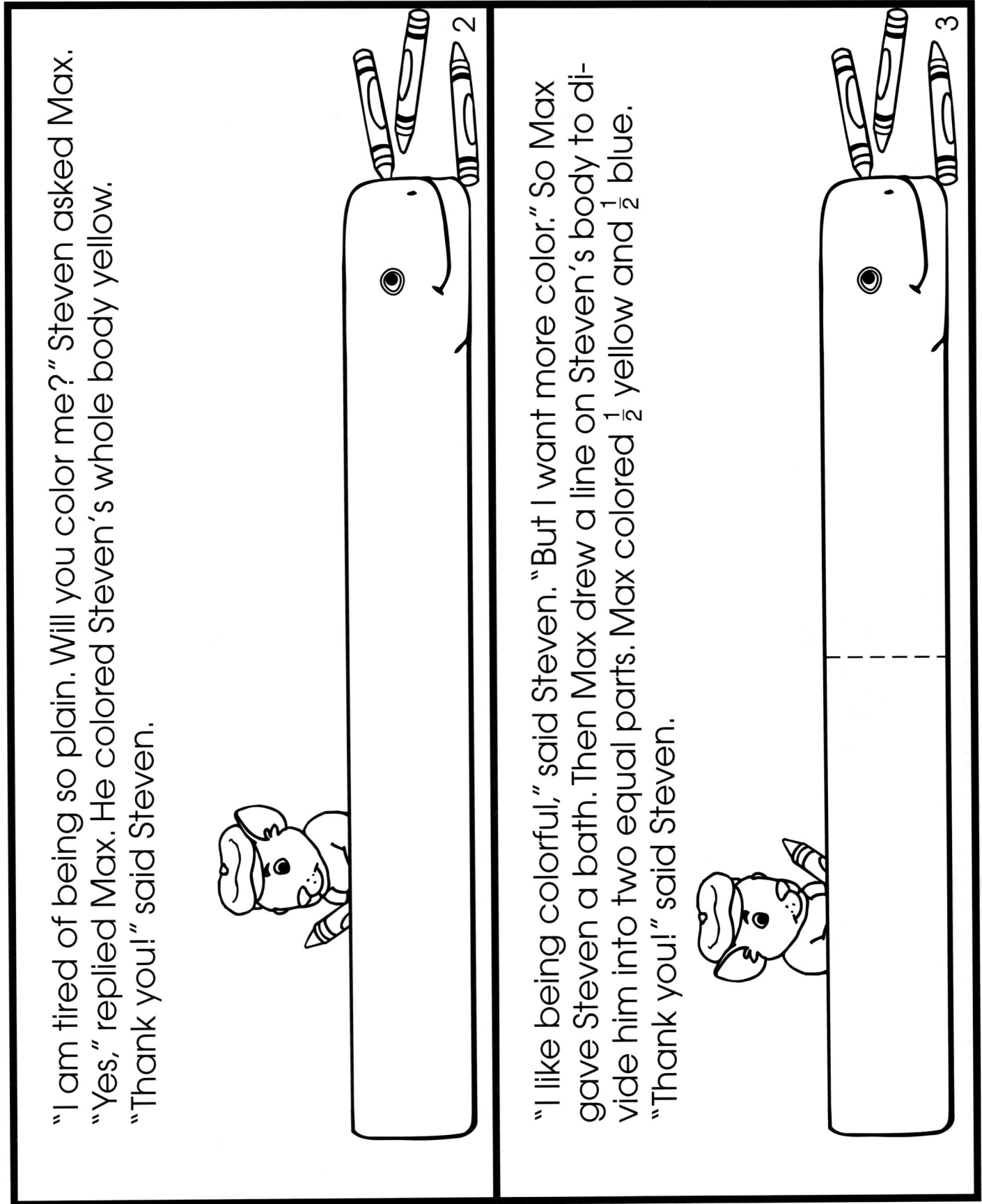

"I am tired of being so plain. Will you color me?" Steven asked Max. "Yes," replied Max. He colored Steven's whole body yellow. "Thank you!" said Steven.

2

"I like being colorful," said Steven. "But I want more color." So Max gave Steven a bath. Then Max drew a line on Steven's body to divide him into two equal parts. Max colored $\frac{1}{2}$ yellow and $\frac{1}{2}$ blue. "Thank you!" said Steven.

3

"I like being two colors," said Steven. "But I want more color." So Max gave Steven another bath. Then Max drew two lines on Steven's body to make three equal parts. Max colored $\frac{1}{3}$ yellow, $\frac{1}{3}$ blue, and $\frac{1}{3}$ green. "Thank you!" said Steven.

4

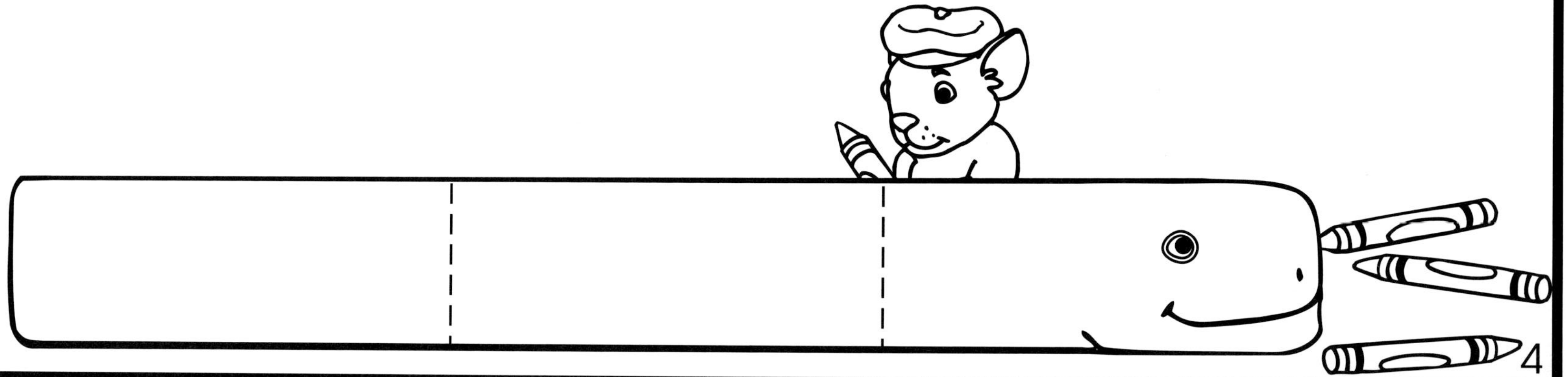

"I like being three colors," said Steven. "But I want even more color." So Max gave Steven another bath. Then Max drew three lines on Steven's body to make four equal parts. Max colored $\frac{1}{4}$ yellow, $\frac{1}{4}$ blue, $\frac{1}{4}$ green, and $\frac{1}{4}$ red. "Perfect!" said Steven. And he lived colorfully ever after.

5

Note to the teacher: Use with "Even Steven" on page 13.

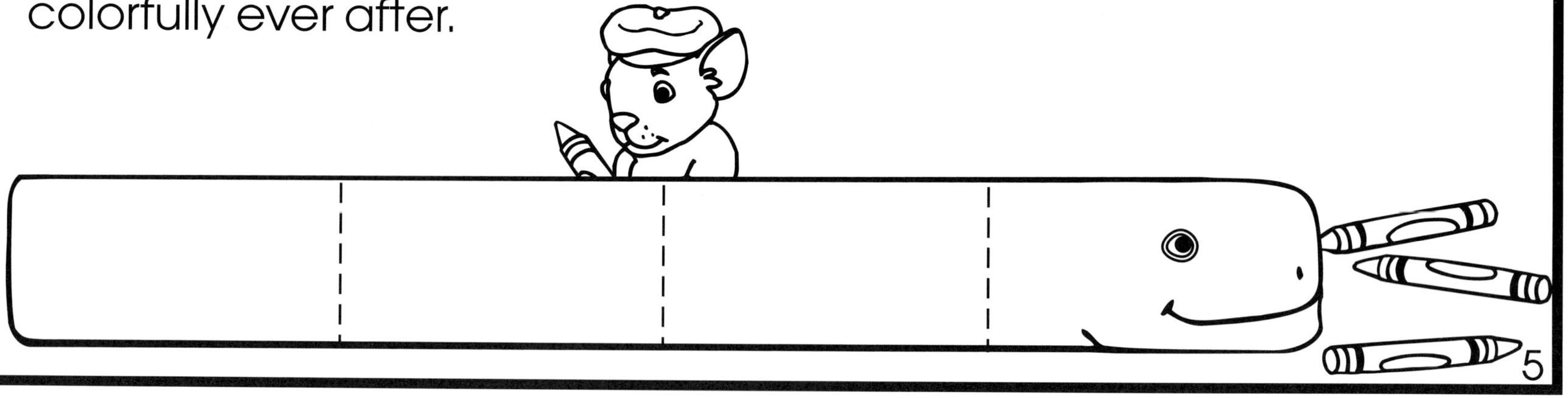

FISHY FRACTIONS

Help your students see that there's nothing fishy about fractions with this fun booklet! Give each student a copy of pages 18–20. Read the pages with students. Then instruct each student to color the cover and booklet pages and cut them out along the bold lines. (Remind students to color lightly over the text so the booklet can be read.) Have each youngster stack his pages in numerical order, place the booklet cover on top, and staple the booklet along the left-hand side as indicated. Provide each student with ten to 12 fish-shaped crackers. Direct him to read each rhyme, use the fish as counters to solve the problem, and then draw the corresponding number of fish on each dish. Tell the student to read the question at the bottom of each booklet page and then write the answer in the blank provided. Let students eat their crackers after completing their booklets. Encourage students to practice reading their booklets with buddies before taking them home to read to their families. That's cool fraction fun!

CREATIVE DECORATING OPTIONS

- Decorate the backing sheet with sequins or pieces of colorful paper.
- Instead of drawing fish, use fish-shaped stickers or fish-shaped stamps.

Extend this booklet by inviting pairs of students to create fraction rhymes. Have each pair write a short math rhyme similar to the rhymes in the booklet. Direct each pair to draw a corresponding picture. Then have one partner write a sentence telling how the items were divided equally. Allow time for each pair to share its rhyme with the class.

Booklet Cover and Page
Cover

Name _____

©The Education Center, Inc.

Perry and Parker Polar Bear
Fish together and always share.
Today's catch is 10 little fish.
Each bear lays **one-half** on his dish.

How many fish are on each dish? _____

©The Education Center, Inc. • *I Can Make It! I Can Read It!* • Math • TEC3520

Sweet Sandy, Sue, and Sonya Seal
Search for a super tasty meal.
They quickly catch 9 little fish.
Then each lays **one-third** on her dish.

How many fish are on each dish? _____

Four penguins—Pat, Paul, Percy, and Pete—
Are in search of a fishy treat.
They catch not 7, but 8 fish.
Then each lays **one-fourth** on his dish.

How many fish are on each dish? _____

Booklet Backing and Page

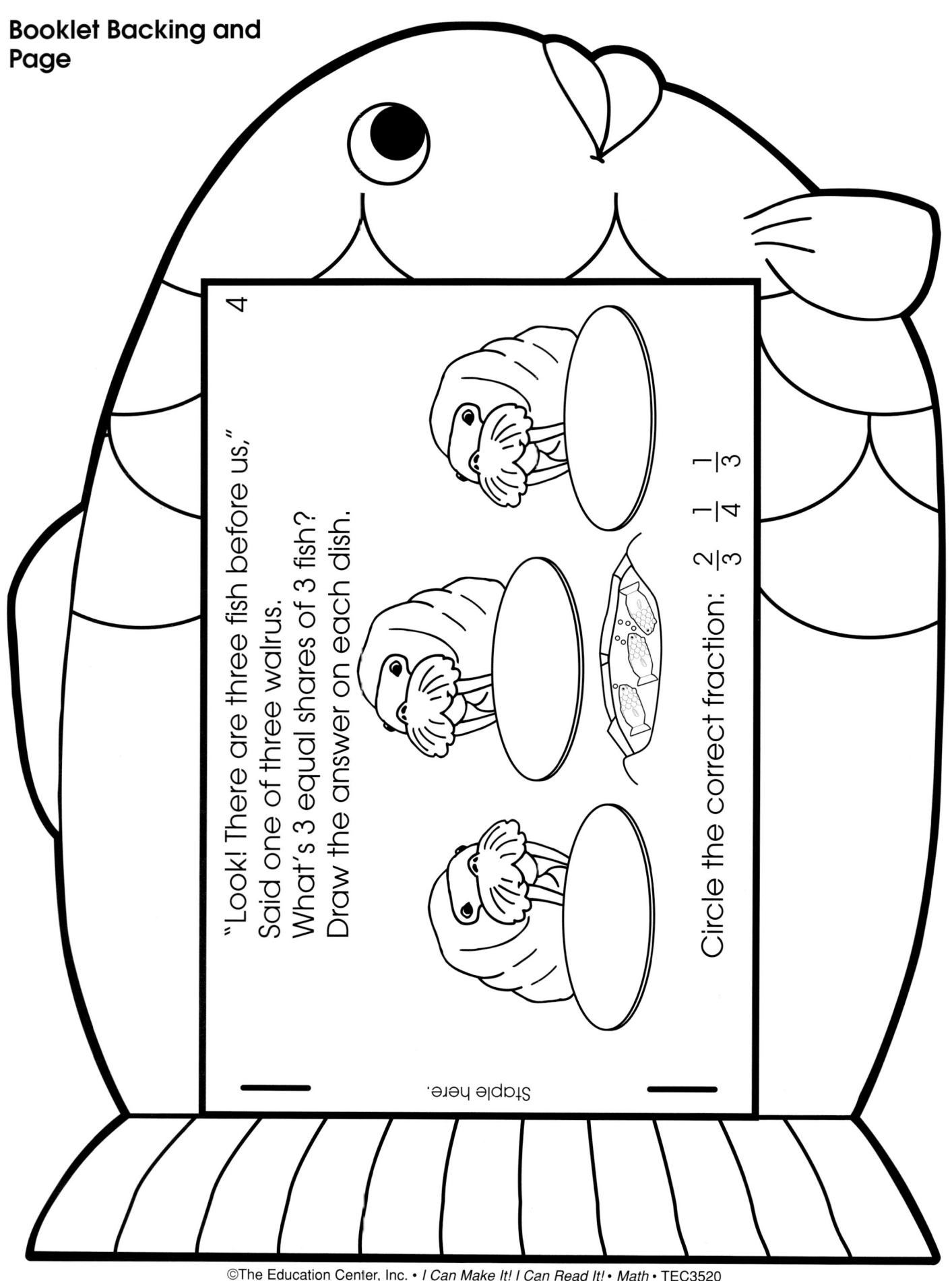

"Look! There are three fish before us,"
Said one of three walrus.
What's 3 equal shares of 3 fish?
Draw the answer on each dish.

Circle the correct fraction: $\frac{2}{3}$ $\frac{1}{4}$ $\frac{1}{3}$

Staple here.

4

HOME, "TWEET" HOME

Students will be all aflutter over using the associative property of addition with this nature-themed booklet. Give each student a copy of page 22 with the counters removed. (Use the counters with the extension activity below.) Then give each student a copy of pages 23–24 and a tongue depressor. Read the booklet pages with students. Instruct each student to color the cover and booklet pages and cut them out along the bold outer lines. (Remind students to color lightly so the text can be read.) Have each youngster stack her pages in numerical order, place the booklet cover on top, and staple the booklet where indicated. Next, have her read each sentence on pages 1–3, draw the number of birds indicated in each empty nest, draw a bow on top of the corresponding number of baby girl birds in each nest, and then complete each number sentence. For page 4, direct each student to choose two numbers for the two sentences. Then have her use the numbers to complete and solve each corresponding number sentence. Instruct the student to draw the correct number of birds in each nest and draw a bow on the corresponding number of baby girl birds. After completing page 4, have each student color the tongue depressor and then glue it to the back of the booklet, as shown, for a tree trunk. Then provide time for each student to practice reading her completed booklet with a classmate. Encourage students to take their booklets home to read to family members. What a special "tweet"!

CREATIVE DECORATING OPTIONS

- Use green tissue paper to decorate the booklet cover.
- Glue pom-poms to the booklet cover for a nest of eggs.

> To extend this booklet activity, provide students with a sheet of paper and the ten counters from page 22. Next, have each student write a different sentence about the number of boy and girl baby birds with a sum of ten or less and its corresponding number sentence. Instruct the student to draw a nest and glue the correct number of baby birds in the nest. Then have her draw a bow on the corresponding number of baby girl birds.

Booklet Cover and Counters

Cover _____ Staple. _____

Home, "Tweet" Home

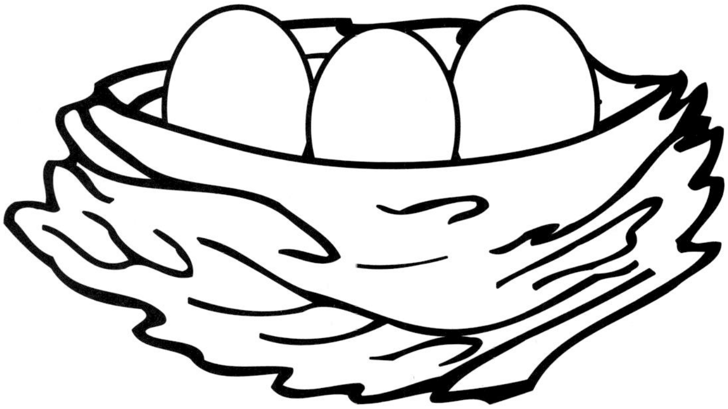

©The Education Center, Inc.

Counters

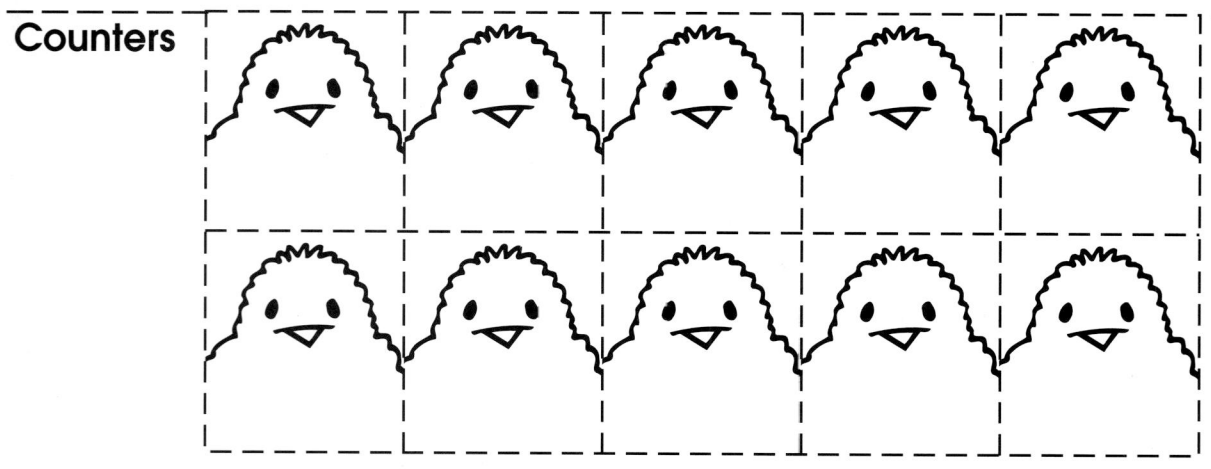

©The Education Center, Inc. • *I Can Make It! I Can Read It!* • Math • TEC3520

Note to the teacher: Use with "Home, 'Tweet' Home" on page 21. Use the counters with the extension activity on page 21.

Booklet Pages

Blue bird family has 3 girls and 1 boy.

3 + 1 = ____

Red bird family has 1 girl and 3 boys.

1 + 3 = ____

1

Yellow bird family has 5 girls and 2 boys.

5 + 2 = ____

Brown bird family has 2 girls and 5 boys.

____ + ____ = ____

2

©The Education Center, Inc. • *I Can Make It! I Can Read It!* • Math • TEC3520

Note to the teacher: Use with "Home, 'Tweet' Home" on page 21.

Booklet Pages

White bird family has 0 girls and 8 boys.

____ + ____ = ____

Purple bird family has 8 girls and 0 boys.

____ + ____ = ____

3

Orange bird family has ____ girls and ____ boys.

____ + ____ = ____

Black bird family has ____ girls and ____ boys.

____ + ____ = ____

4

PARROTS, MONKEYS, AND ANTS, OH MY!

Use this minibooklet activity to provide your youngsters with a rain forest counting adventure. Give each student a white construction paper copy of pages 26–28 and three paper clips. To make the parrot booklet, have each student count the parrots on each page by 2s and then write the corresponding total in the box located in the upper right-hand corner of each page. Have students color the parrots as desired. Remind students to complete and color the last booklet page, which is found on the booklet backing (page 28). To assemble the booklet, direct each student to cut out the booklet cover and pages along the bold and dotted lines. Have him sequence the pages and lay them end to end. Instruct the student to glue the cutouts together where indicated to create one long strip. When the glue is dry, help each child accordion-fold his booklet. Next, help him glue the minibooklet to the booklet backing (page 28) where indicated. Direct students to follow the same process to complete the monkey and ant booklets. Have each youngster practice reading his completed minibooklets; then encourage him to take the set home to read with family members. Direct him to use a paper clip to keep each booklet closed. What a creative counting review!

CREATIVE DECORATING OPTIONS

- Use fluorescent crayons or chalk to color the parrots.
- Help students paint the sky portions of their booklet pages with thinned blue paint.

To extend this booklet activity, invite a group of student volunteers to act out one minibooklet. Continue this process with a different group until each booklet has been acted out.

Parrot Booklet Cover and Pages

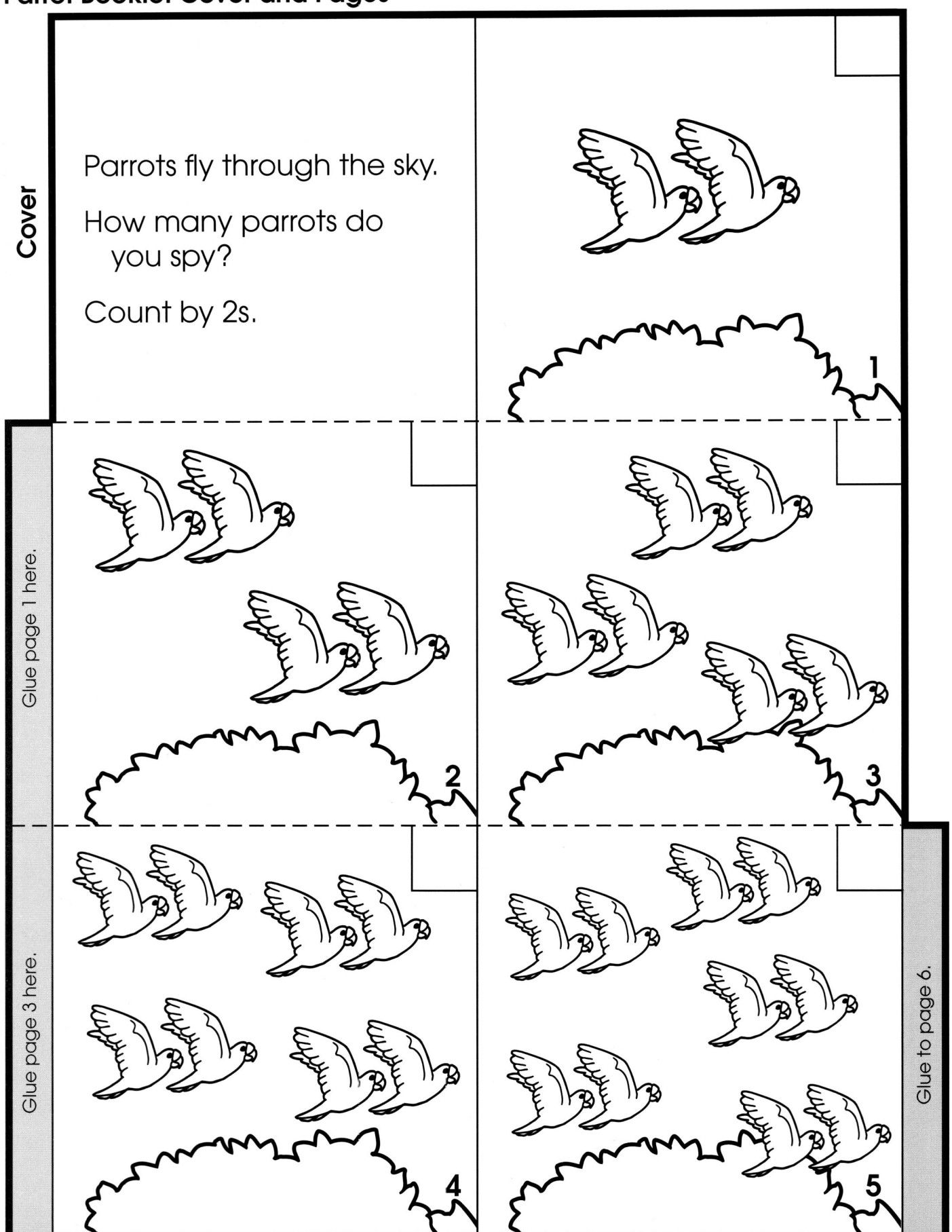

Cover

Parrots fly through the sky.

How many parrots do you spy?

Count by 2s.

Glue page 1 here.

Glue page 3 here.

Glue to page 6.

©The Education Center, Inc. • *I Can Make It! I Can Read It!* • Math • TEC3520

Note to the teacher: Use with "Parrots, Monkeys, and Ants, Oh My!" on page 25.

Monkey and Ant Booklet Covers and Pages

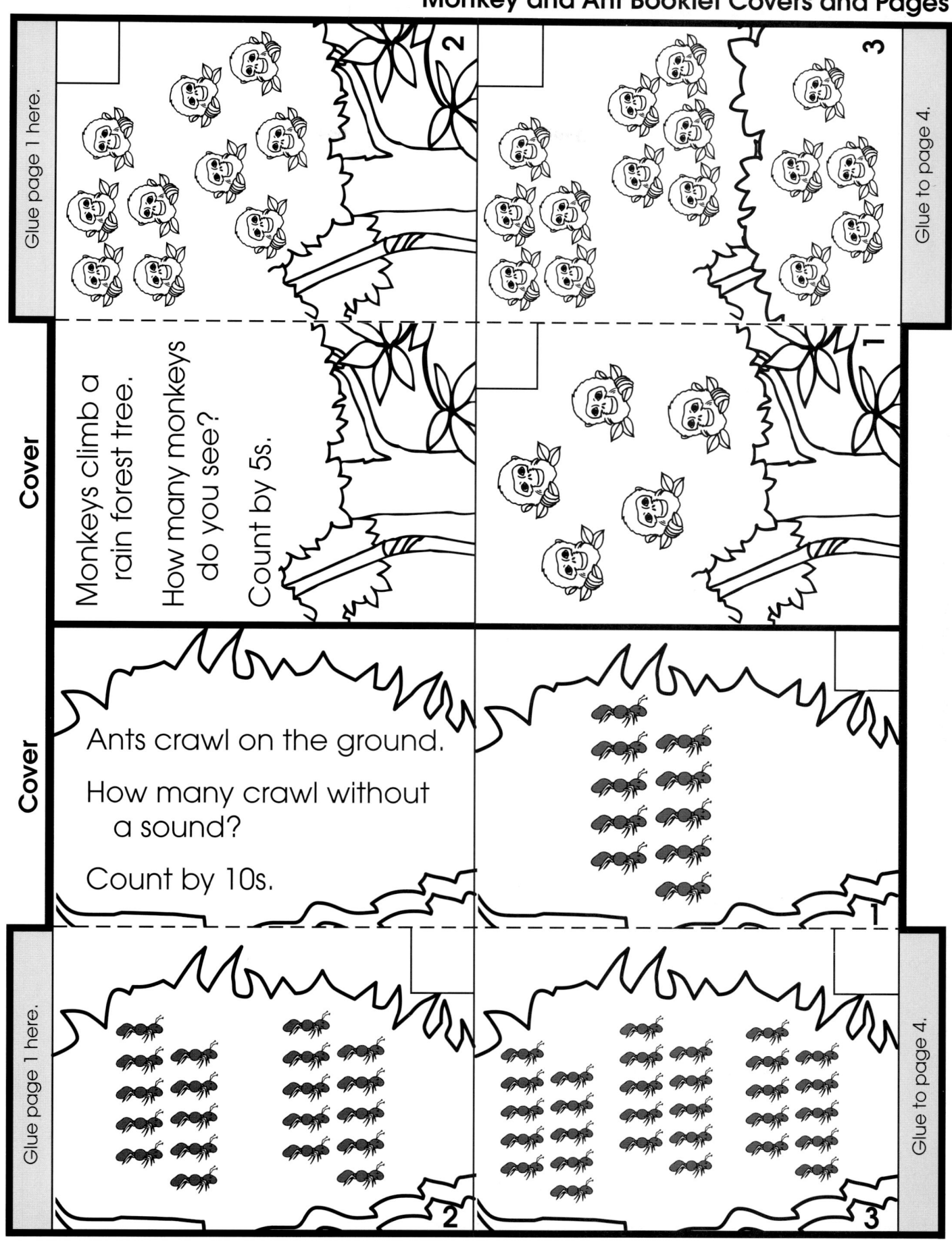

Cover: Monkeys climb a rain forest tree. How many monkeys do you see? Count by 5s.

Cover: Ants crawl on the ground. How many crawl without a sound? Count by 10s.

Booklet Backing and Pages

Rain forest animals,

Rain forest plants,

How many parrots, monkeys, and ants?

by

Name

©The Education Center, Inc. • *I Can Make It! I Can Read It!* • Math • TEC3520

Note to the teacher: Use with "Parrots, Monkeys, and Ants, Oh My!" on page 25.

DELIGHTFUL DRAGONFLIES

With this delightful dragonfly booklet, your students will be all abuzz writing number sentences to solve word problems! Give each student a copy of pages 30–33. Read the booklet pages with students. Instruct each student to color the cover, the booklet pages, and the booklet backing and cut them out along the bold outer lines. (Remind students to color lightly so the text can be read.) Have each youngster lay her booklet pages in numerical order across her work surface. Next, have the student read the first word problem, draw the corresponding sets of dragonflies on the correct blank wing of the booklet backing, and then write the number sentence in the space provided. After completing the word problem, have her glue the wing as shown. Direct students to follow the same process with each remaining wing. After the glue has dried, help each student staple her cover as shown. Provide time for each student to practice reading her completed booklet with a classmate. Encourage students to take their booklets home to read to family members.

CREATIVE DECORATING OPTIONS

- Sponge-paint each wing with thinned yellow paint.
- Use glitter for the eyes.

Extend this activity by introducing your students to the fact family used in the booklet's word problems. Display the addition sentence 6 + 7 = 13. Explain that this addition fact is a part of a fact family of four members. Write the three remaining members (facts) on the board (7 + 6 = 13, 13 – 6 = 7, 13 – 7 = 6). Use Unifix cubes to demonstrate the four facts. Guide students in understanding that fact families are addition and subtraction facts that use the same three numbers.

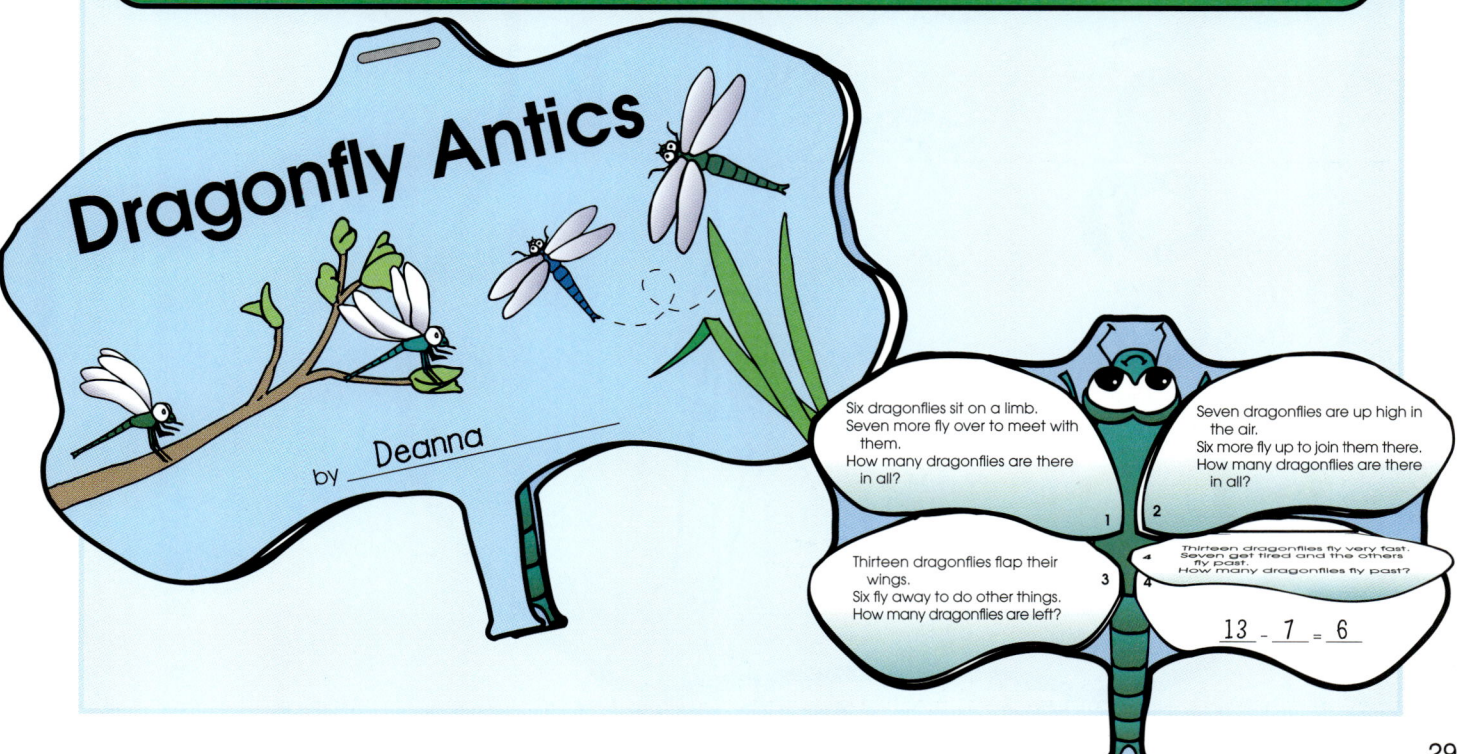

Booklet Cover

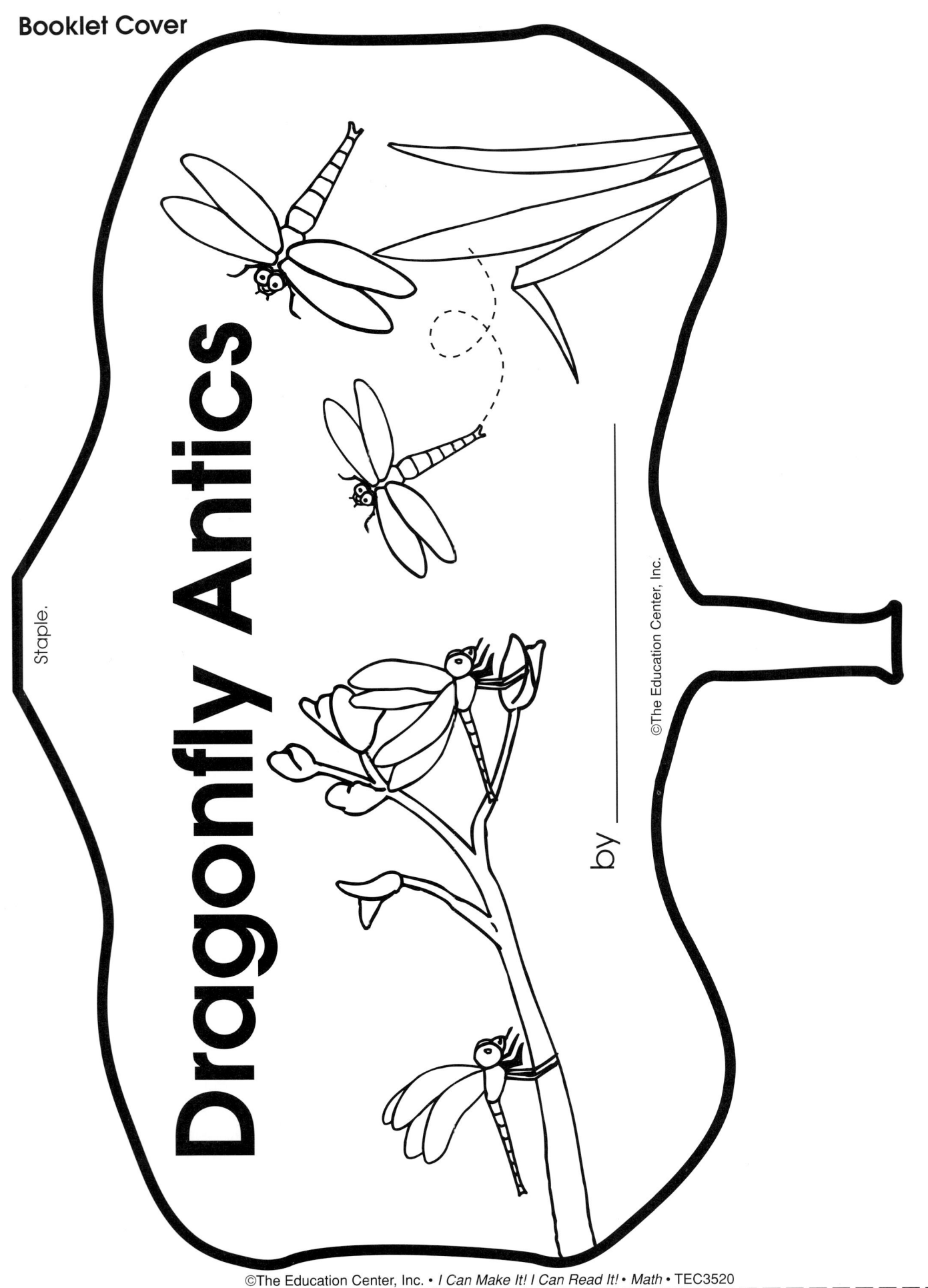

Six dragonflies sit on a limb.
Seven more fly over to meet with them.
How many dragonflies are there in all?

1

Seven dragonflies are up high in the air.
Six more fly up to join them there.
How many dragonflies are there in all?

2

Note to the teacher: Use with "Delightful Dragonflies" on page 29.

Booklet Pages

Thirteen dragonflies flap their wings.
Six fly away to do other things.
How many dragonflies are left?

3

4

Thirteen dragonflies fly very fast.
Seven get tired and the others fly past.
How many dragonflies fly past?

Booklet Backing

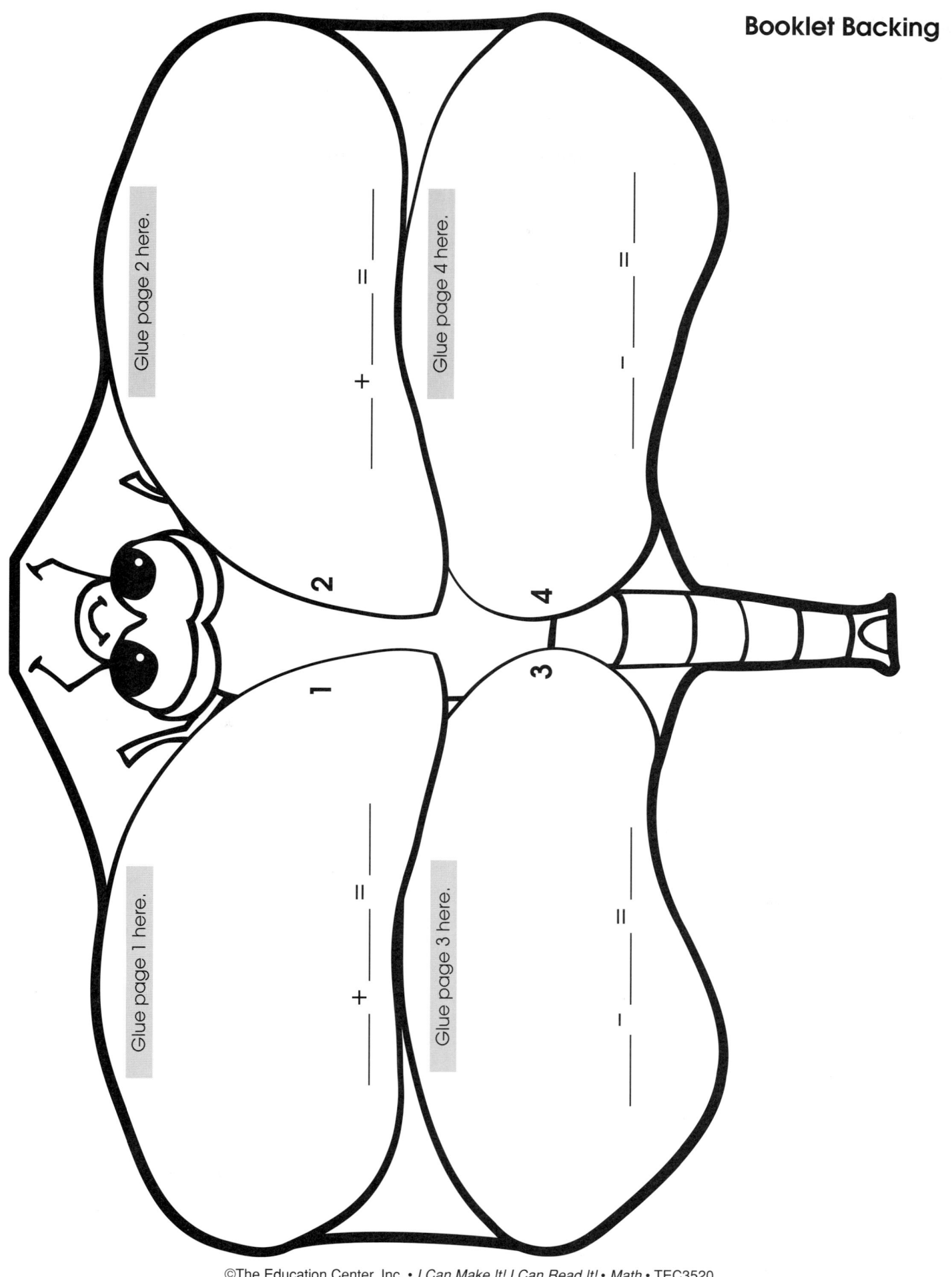

©The Education Center, Inc. • *I Can Make It! I Can Read It!* • Math • TEC3520

Note to the teacher: Use with "Delightful Dragonflies" on page 29.

PETS GALORE

Help students identify attributes with this fun pet-shop booklet activity! Give each student a copy of pages 35–38. Read the booklet pages with students. Then instruct each student to color and cut out his cover, booklet pages, backing page, and booklet animal patterns. (Remind students to color lightly over the text so the pages can be read.) To complete the booklet, have each youngster read the clues on each page and then glue the corresponding animal(s) in the center of the page. Help the student stack pages 1–3 and then staple them to page 4 where indicated. Have him glue the sides of the cover to the backing page where indicated. Then have the student cut along the dotted lines to separate the doors for the cover. After the glue has dried, invite each student to read his completed booklet with a partner before taking it home to share with family members.

CREATIVE DECORATING OPTION

- Use colored chalk to color each animal.

To extend this booklet activity, invite each student to imagine and then draw a picture of a one-of-a-kind pet he would like to have. Tell students to write a descriptive sentence about their pets.

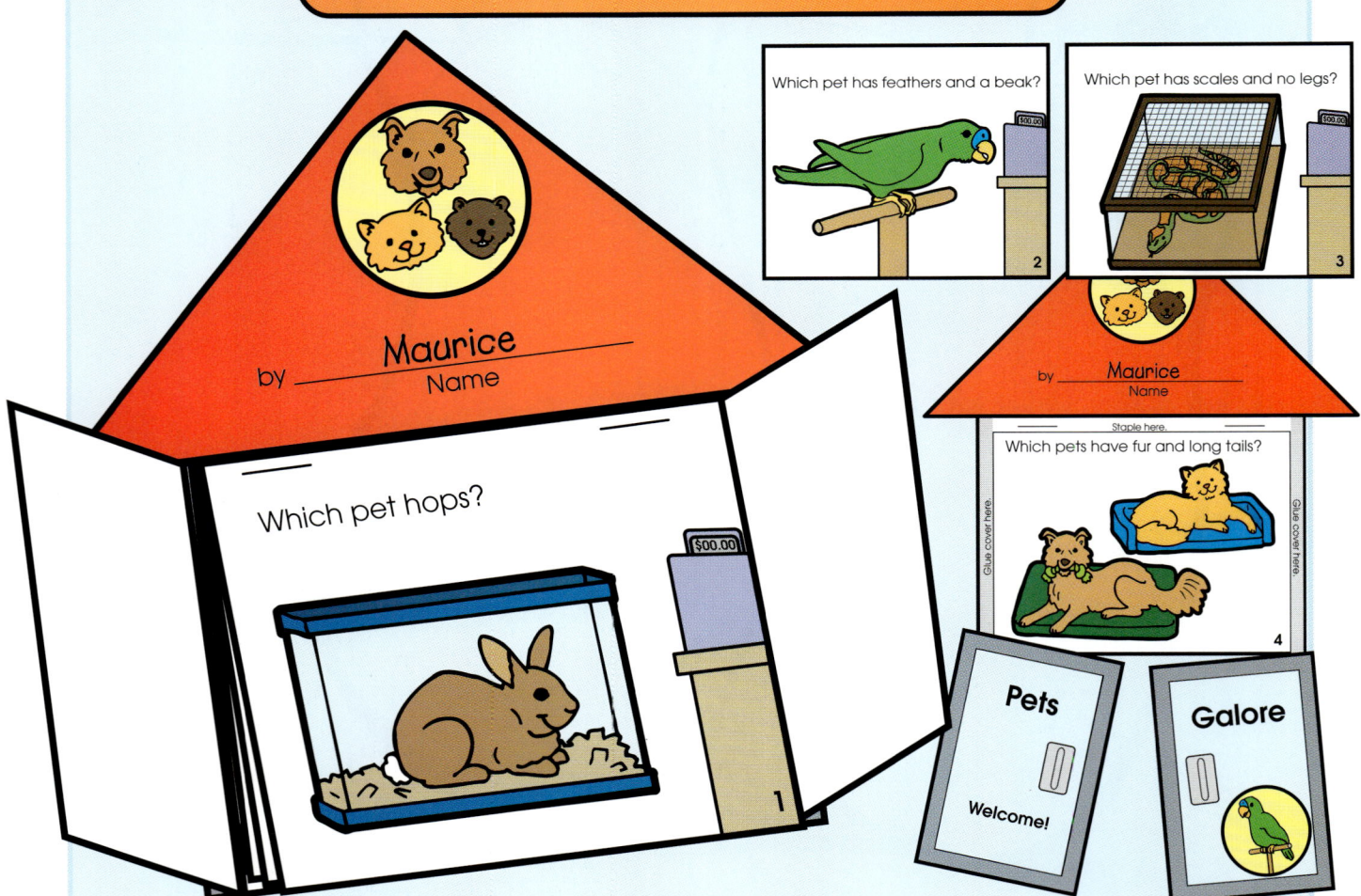

Cover and Booklet Page

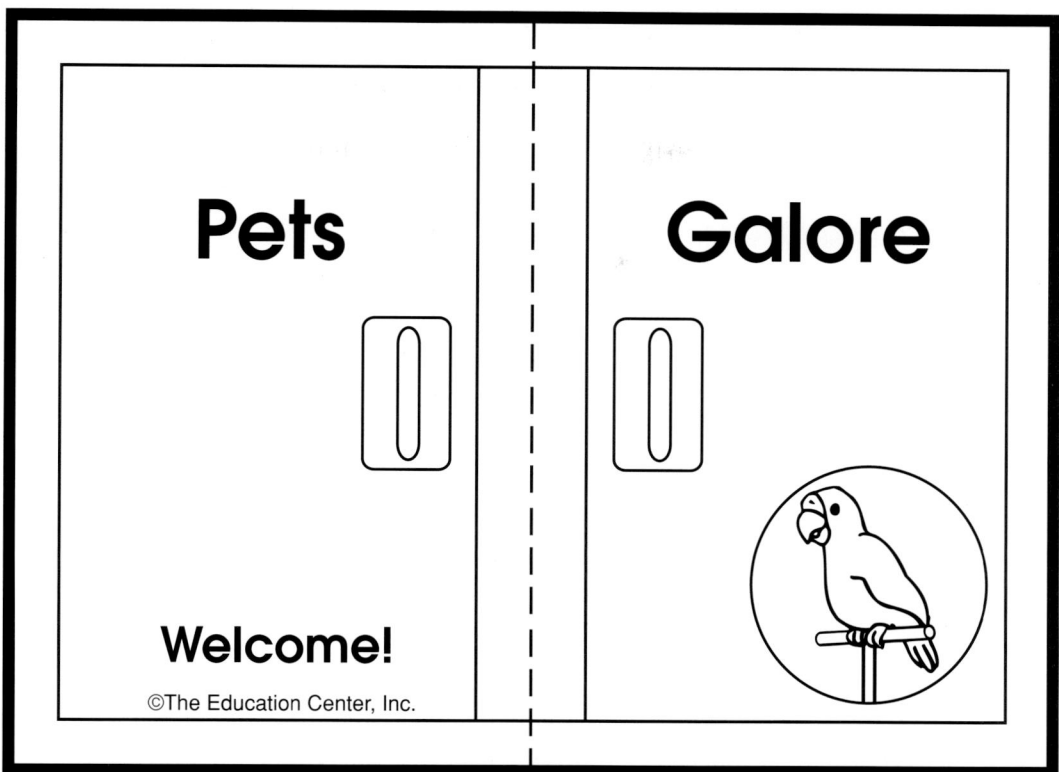

Welcome!
©The Education Center, Inc.

Cover

Which pet hops?

1

©The Education Center, Inc. • *I Can Make It! I Can Read It!* • Math • TEC3520

Booklet Pages

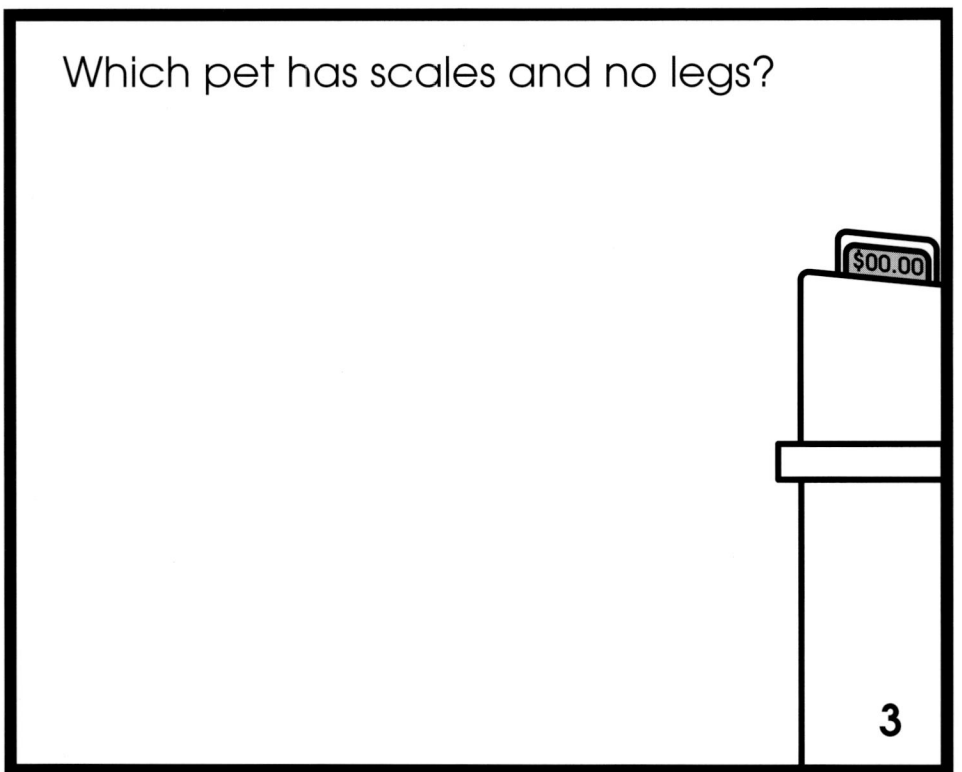

©The Education Center, Inc. • *I Can Make It! I Can Read It!* • *Math* • TEC3520

Note to the teacher: Use with "Pets Galore" on page 34.

Booklet Backing Page

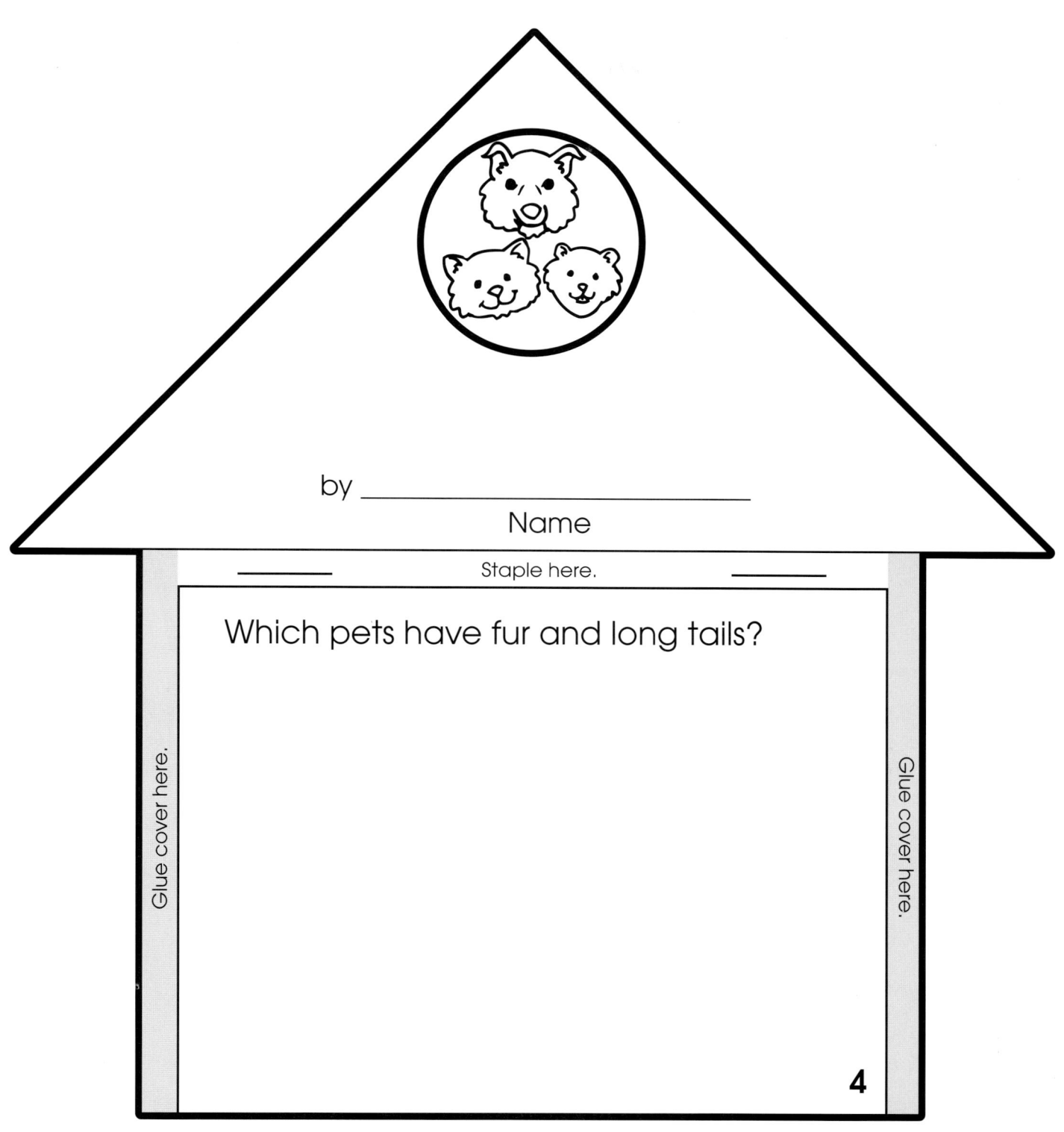

by _____
Name

Staple here.

Which pets have fur and long tails?

Glue cover here.

Glue cover here.

4

©The Education Center, Inc. • *I Can Make It! I Can Read It!* • Math • TEC3520

Note to the teacher: Use with "Pets Galore" on page 34.

Animal Patterns

KANGA MAKES A PATTERN

Reinforce patterning skills with this rollicking booklet activity! Give each student a copy of pages 40–43. Read the cover and pattern cards with students. Instruct each student to color the cover, booklet pages, and movement cards and cut them out on the bold lines. (Remind students to color lightly so the text can be read.) Next, have each youngster sequence her cutouts in numerical order and lay them end to end. Instruct the student to glue the booklet pages together where indicated to create one long strip; then have her glue booklet page 8 to the backing page. Instruct the student to personalize the cover. Next, help each student accordion-fold the pages as shown. Direct the student to stack and then lay the movement cards beside Mother Kangaroo. Then divide students into pairs. In turn, have each partner unfold her booklet. Instruct the student to lay four movement cards on the first four booklet pages to create a desired pattern similar to the one shown. Have Partner 2 use her own movement cards to extend the pattern on booklet pages 5–8. After each partner has had a turn, have her place her movement cards inside Mother Kangaroo's pouch behind page 8. Encourage students to take their booklets home to read to family members. Your youngsters are sure to want to repeat this activity again and again!

CREATIVE DECORATING OPTIONS

- Sponge-paint Mother Kangaroo and each Kanga pattern with brown paint.
- Glue wiggle eyes on Mother Kangaroo and each Kanga pattern.

To extend this activity, have each youngster use crayons to draw her favorite pattern on her booklet pages.

Booklet Backing Page and Cover

Backing Page

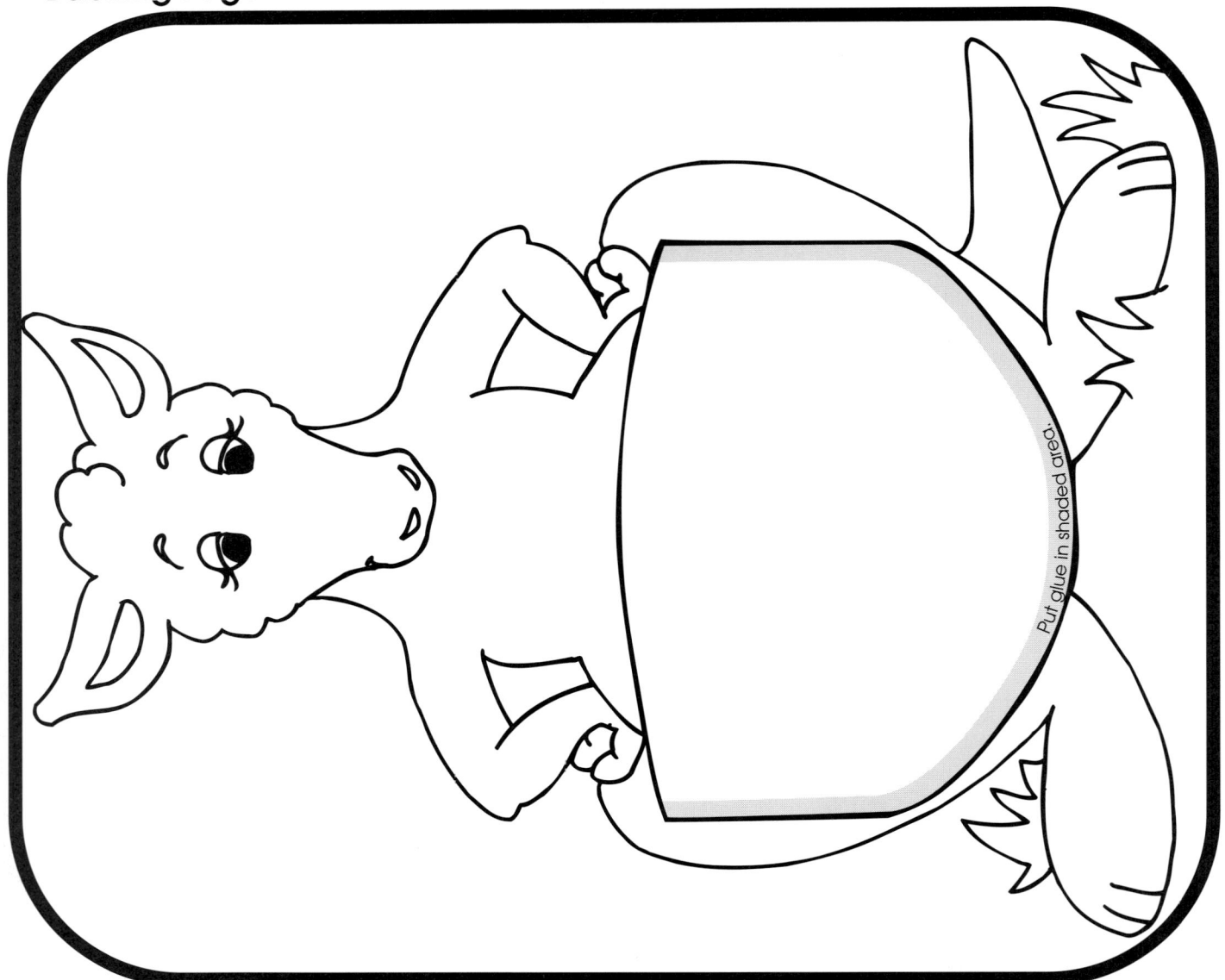

Cover

Kanga Makes a Pattern

Kanga moves this way and that,
Moving like an acrobat.
Hop, twist, stomp, and clap,
Kanga makes a pattern—
Just like that!

by _____

Booklet Pages

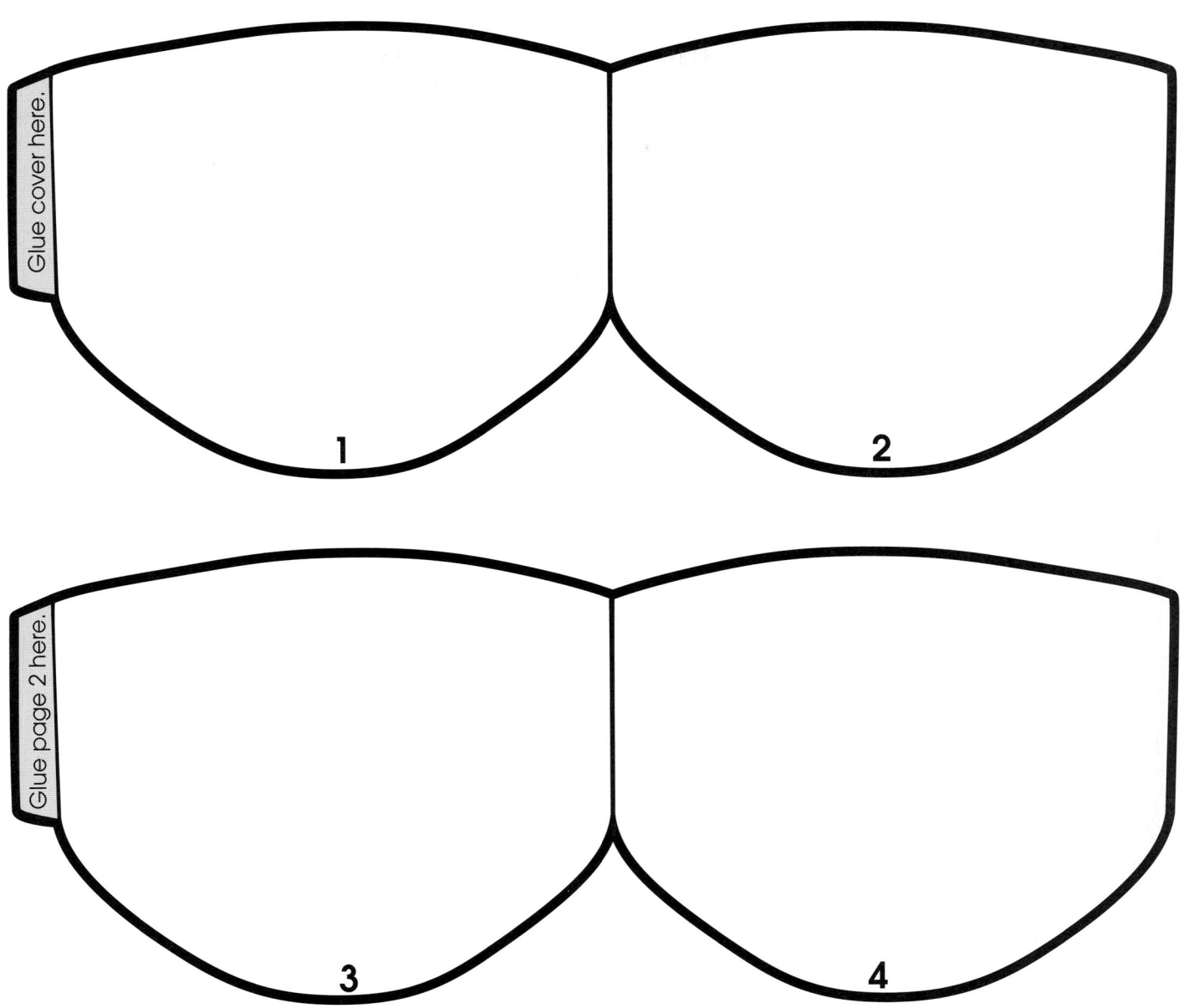

©The Education Center, Inc. • *I Can Make It! I Can Read It!* • Math • TEC3520

Note to the teacher: Use with "Kanga Makes a Pattern" on page 39.

Booklet Pages

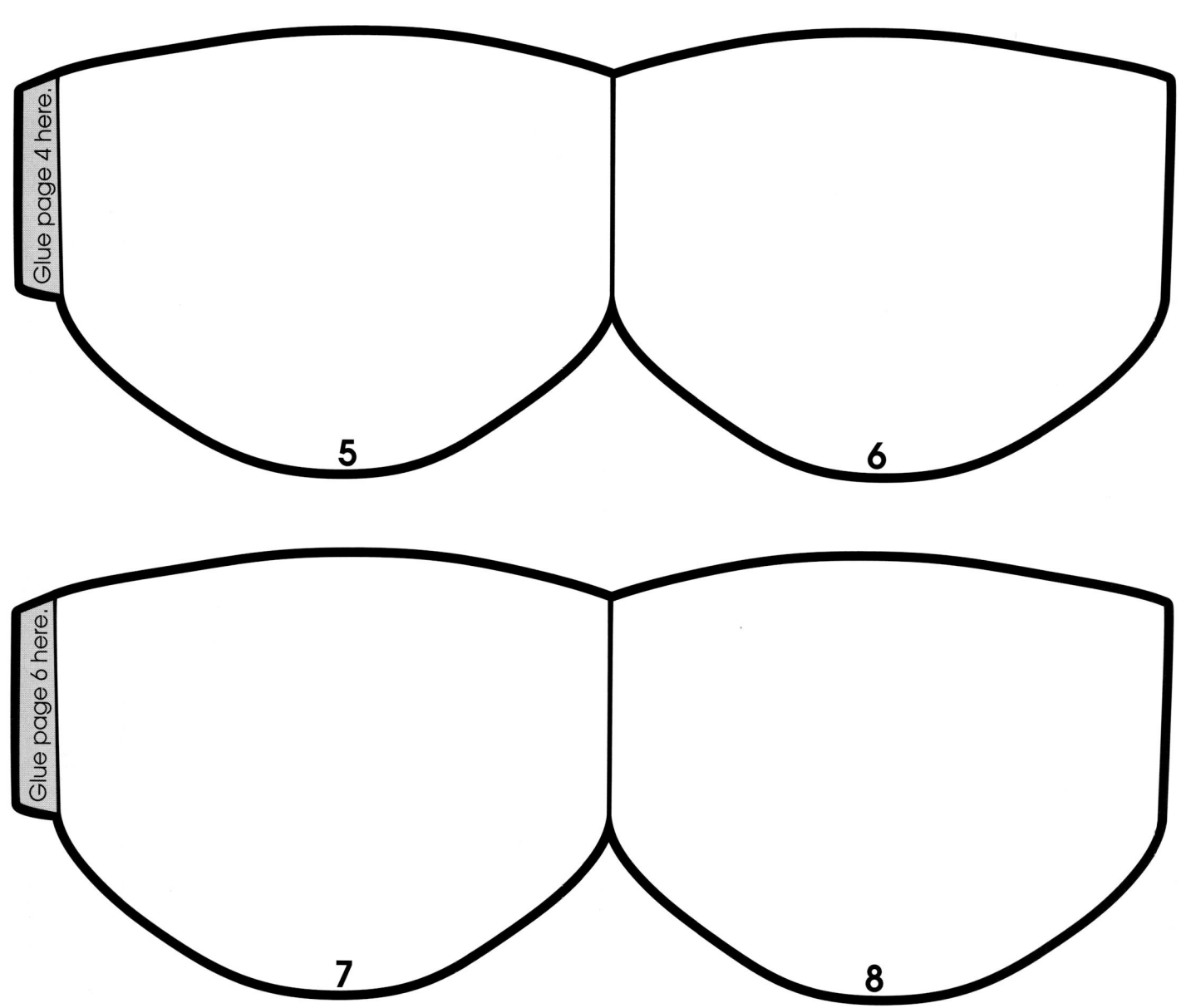

Movement Cards

SHEP'S SHAPES

Let Shep help your students "bone up" on plane figures with this hands-on booklet activity! Give each student a copy of pages 45–48. Read the booklet pages with students. Then instruct each student to color his cover and backing page and cut them out along the bold lines. (Do not have students color the shapes on the backing page at this point.) Next, have students cut out the clue pages (page 46) and the blank pages (page 47). Direct students to stack their clue pages in random order; then help the students staple the pages to the backing page where indicated. Then have students stack the blank pages and staple them to the backing page where indicated. Next, have each youngster cut out each shape label (page 48) and glue it below its corresponding shape on the backing page. Tell him to color and cut out each shape on page 45. Then have the student color each shape's mate on the backing page the same color. Next, instruct the student to read each clue page, glue the corresponding shape cutout to the blank page, and then write the shape's name on the blank provided. Then help the student staple the cover as shown. Encourage each student to read his completed booklet with a partner before taking it home to share with his family. What a "paw-fect" review of shapes and their attributes!

CREATIVE DECORATING OPTION

- Use bright watercolors instead of crayons.

To extend this booklet activity, invite each student to write a shape clue on the back of his booklet. Have student partners trade booklets and solve each clue by drawing the corresponding shape below it. Instruct each student to check his partner's answer.

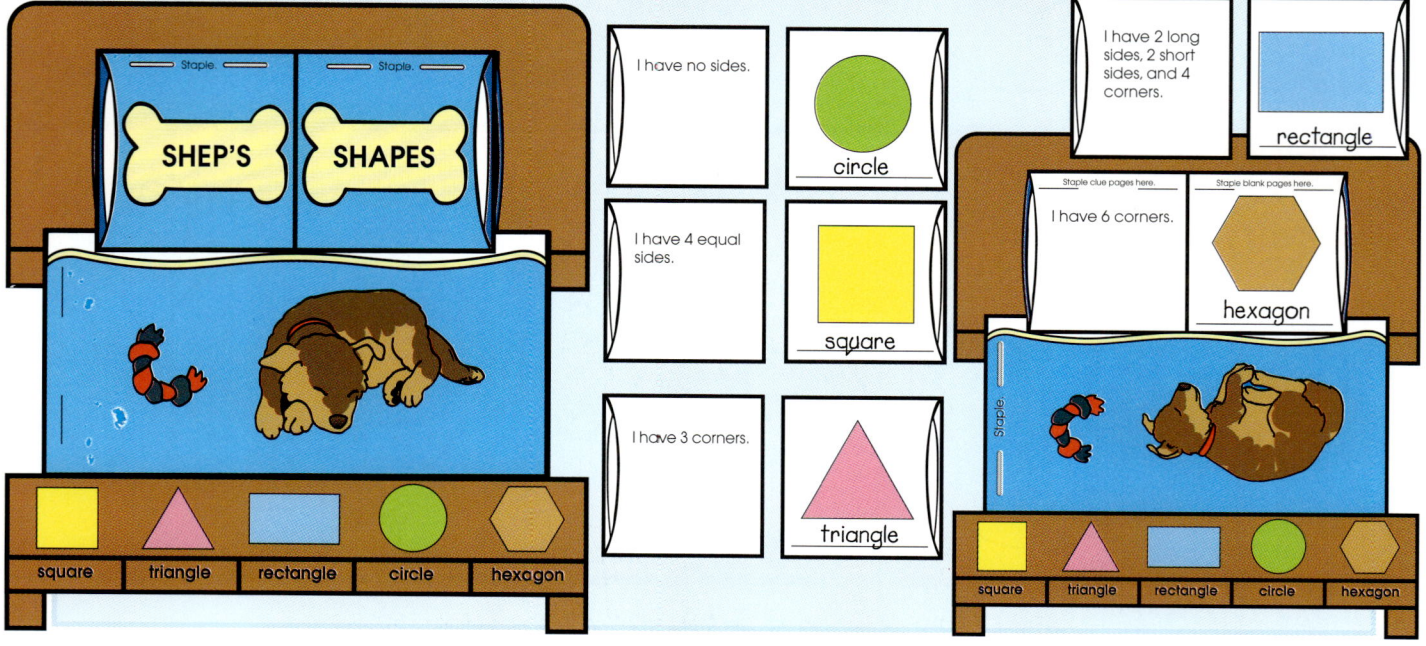

Booklet Cover and Shape Patterns

Cover

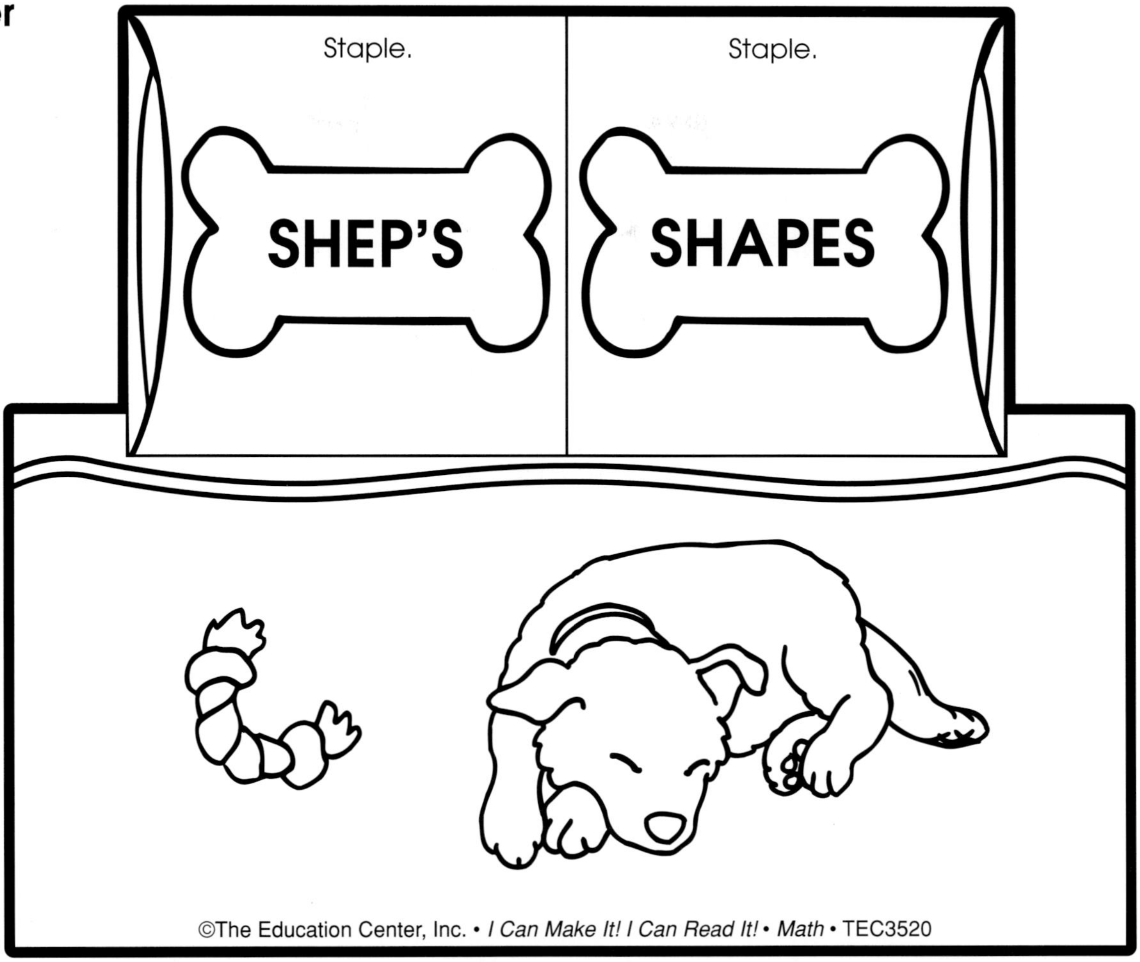

Staple. Staple.

SHEP'S SHAPES

©The Education Center, Inc. • *I Can Make It! I Can Read It!* • Math • TEC3520

Shapes

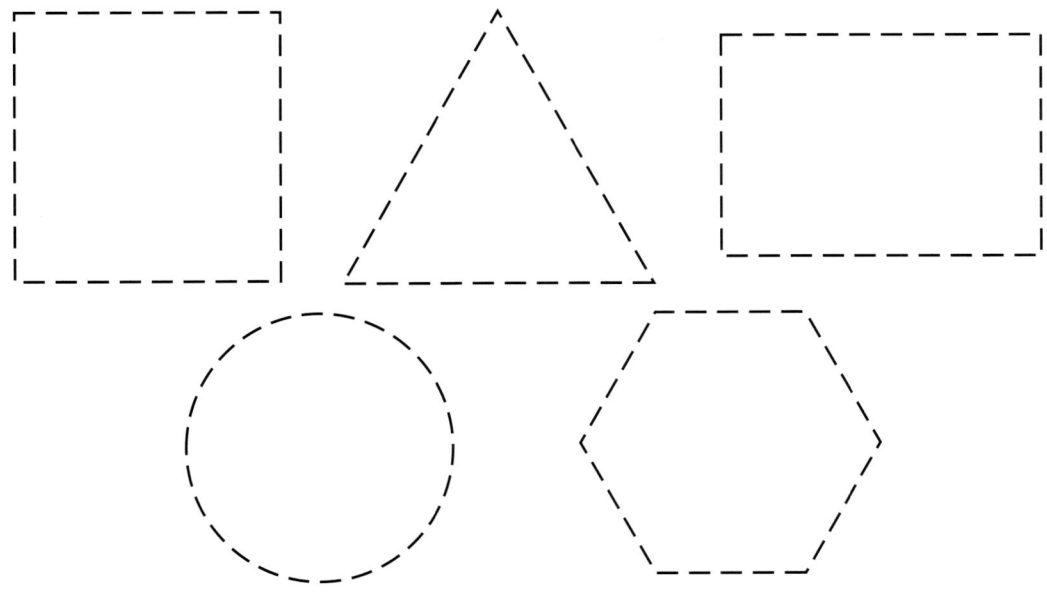

©The Education Center, Inc. • *I Can Make It! I Can Read It!* • Math • TEC3520

Note to the teacher: Use with "Shep's Shapes" on page 44.

45

Clue Pages

I have no sides.	I have 4 equal sides.
I have 3 corners.	I have 2 long sides, 2 short sides, and 4 corners.

Blank Pages

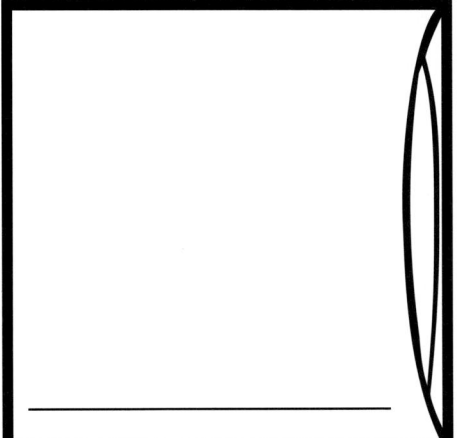
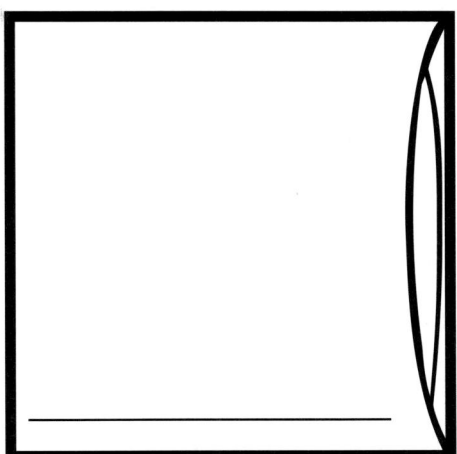

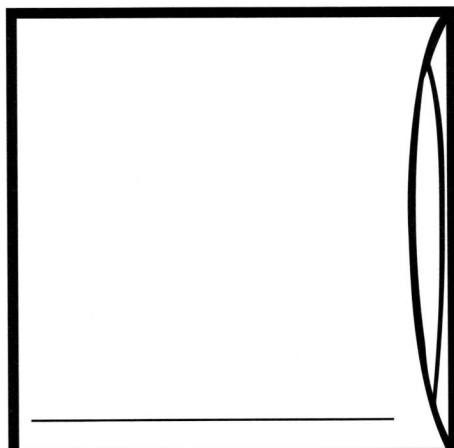

©The Education Center, Inc. • *I Can Make It! I Can Read It!* • Math • TEC3520

Note to the teacher: Use with "Shep's Shapes" on page 44.

Booklet Backing Page and Shape Labels

Shape Labels

| circle | triangle | hexagon | square | rectangle |

FROG'S BUSY DAY

Location, location, location! Use this interactive booklet to help students better understand relative positions as well as help busy Frog review his day. Give each student one brad and a copy of pages 50–53. Have each student color the booklet backing and top wheel and cut them out along the bold lines. Then have her cut out the middle and bottom wheels. For the top wheel, instruct each student to cut out the top of each section along the dotted lines. Next, help the student insert a brad through the center holes, first through the top wheel, the middle wheel, the bottom wheel, and then the booklet backing. To use the booklet, the student aligns the top of section 1 of the top wheel with Frog's head. She then determines and aligns the word on the middle wheel that best identifies the frog's location in the picture. Next, the student decides which sentence on the bottom wheel best describes the picture and aligns it with section 1 and the middle wheel. The student continues in this manner with sections 2–6. Now that's a "wheely" great reading and math activity!

CREATIVE DECORATING OPTION

- Use green tempera paint, glitter, or sequins to decorate the frog.

To extend this booklet activity, have each student draw herself on a separate sheet of paper in her favorite scene from the booklet. Then have the student write a sentence to describe what she is doing in the picture.

Booklet Backing

50 **Note to the teacher:** Use with "Frog's Busy Day" on page 49.

Booklet Pattern

Top Wheel

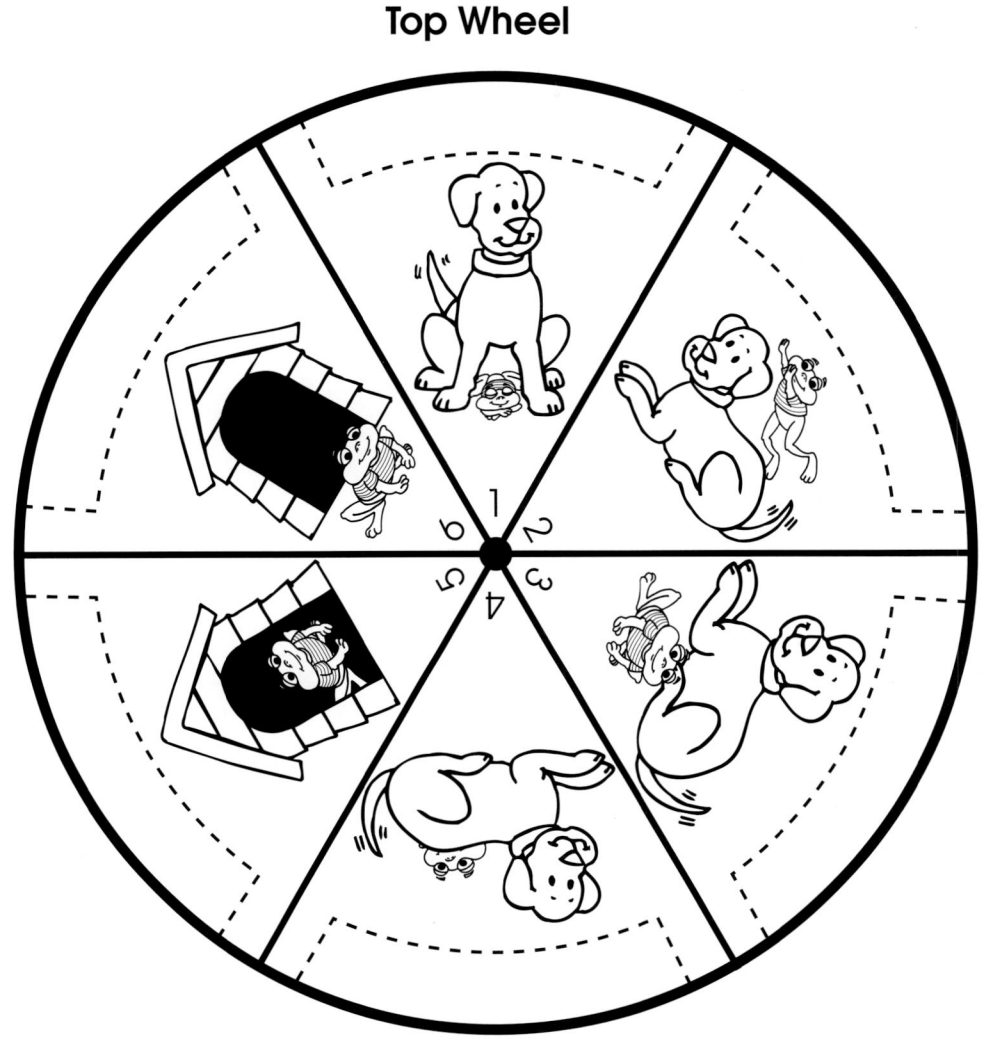

©The Education Center, Inc. • *I Can Make It! I Can Read It!* • Math • TEC3520

Note to the teacher: Use with "Frog's Busy Day" on page 49.

Booklet Pattern

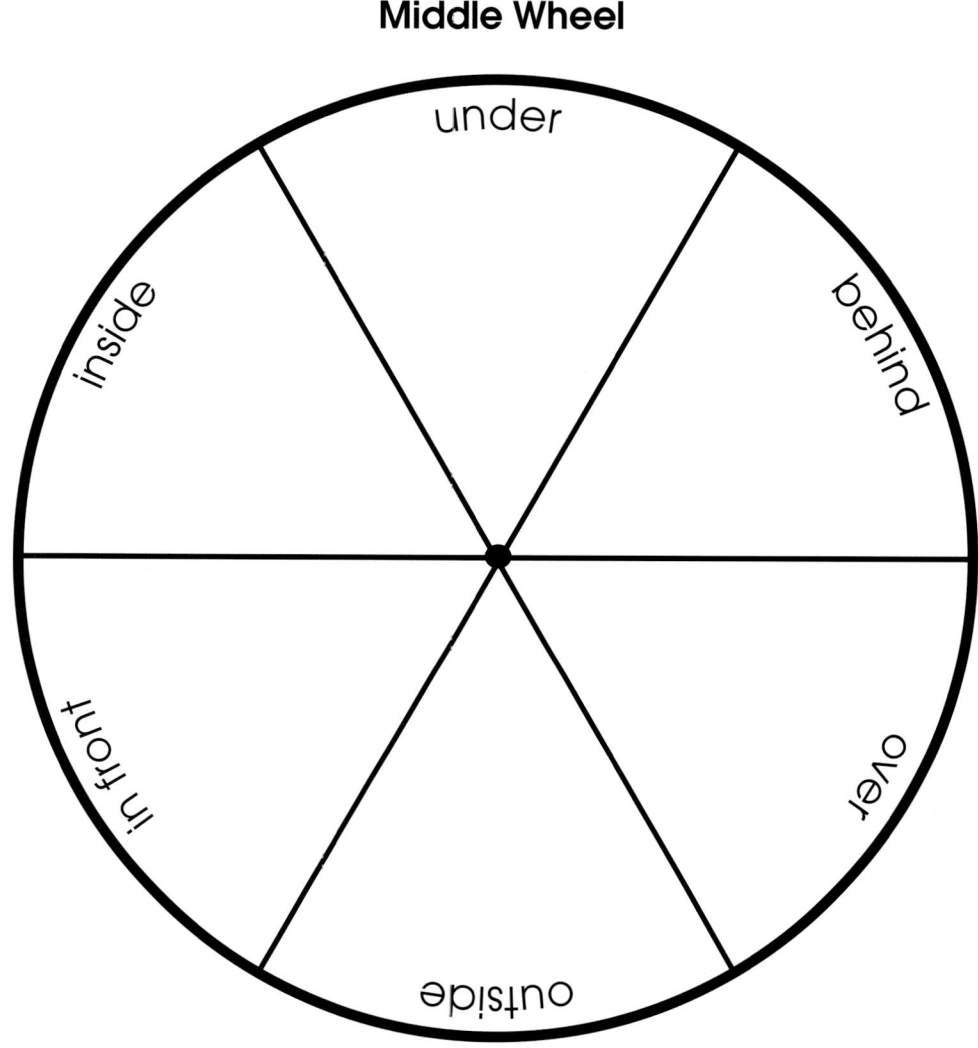

Middle Wheel

Booklet Pattern

Bottom Wheel

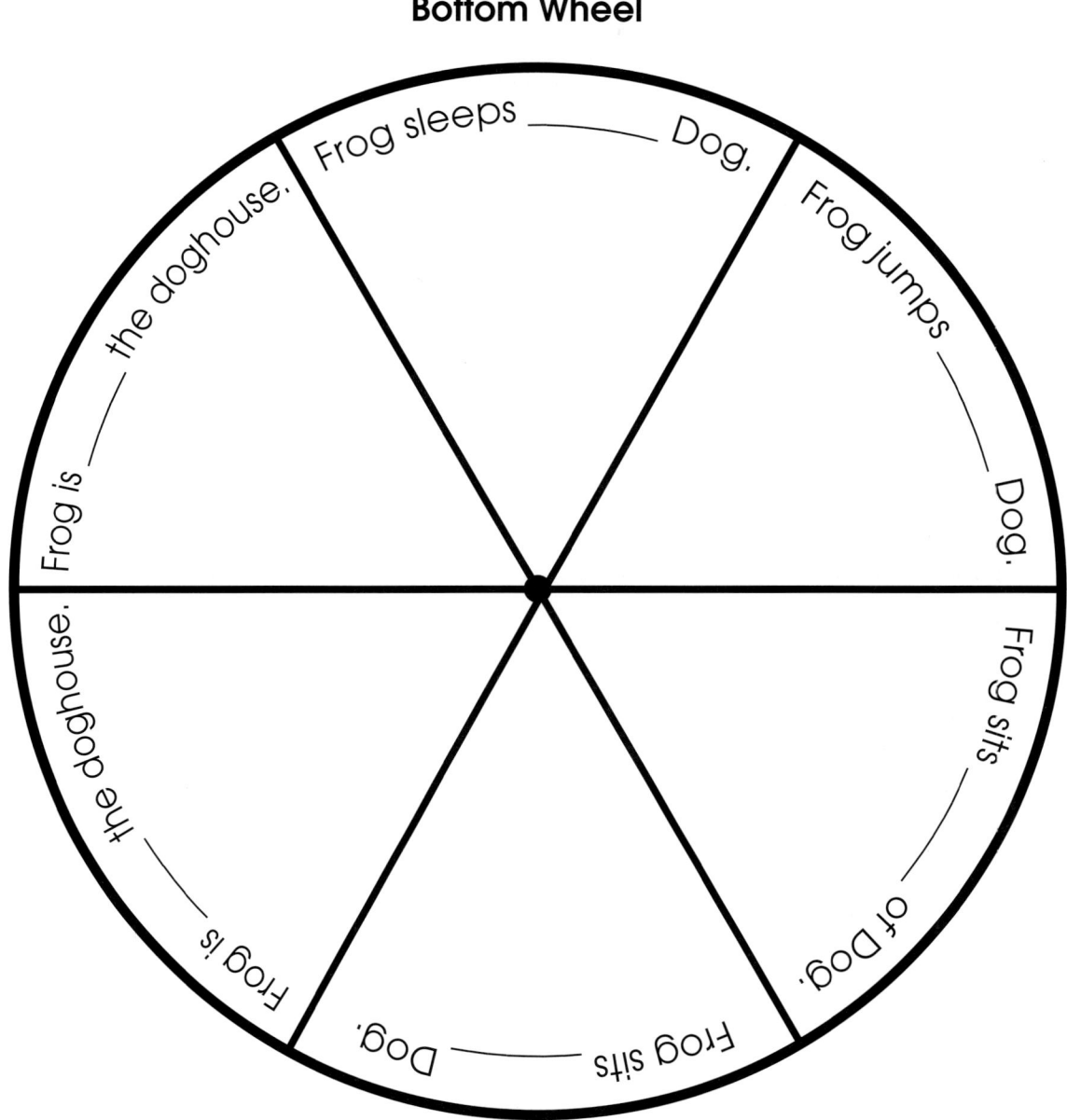

SALLY'S SHAPES

Help your students identify solid figures with this "seal-sational" booklet activity! Give each student a copy of pages 55–58 and a 6" x 14" sheet of colored construction paper. Read the booklet pages with students. Direct each student to cut out the cover, solid figure patterns, sea lion pattern, and booklet pages along the bold lines. Then instruct the student to color the cover, solid figure patterns, and sea lion pattern. Next, have him glue each solid figure pattern on its corresponding booklet page. Direct the student to read the question at the bottom of each page and then color the correct answer. Tell the student to stack his pages in numerical order, place the cover on top, and staple the booklet to the top of the construction paper as shown. Then have him glue Sally to the construction paper as shown. Encourage students to practice reading their booklets with buddies before taking them home to read to their families. Watch your youngsters successfully juggle solid figures!

CREATIVE DECORATING OPTION

- Use crayons to draw a scene around Sally. For example, draw the sea lion pool and demonstration area at a zoo.

To extend this booklet, give students discarded magazines and circulars and direct them to search for and cut out pictures of solid figures that correspond with the booklet. Then have each student glue the pictures to the back of his construction paper and label them.

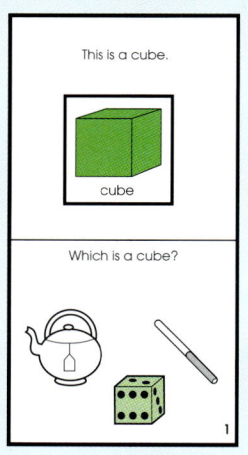
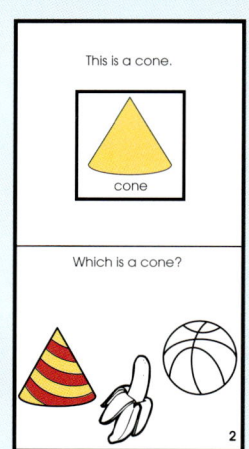
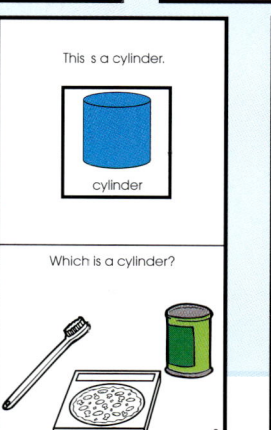
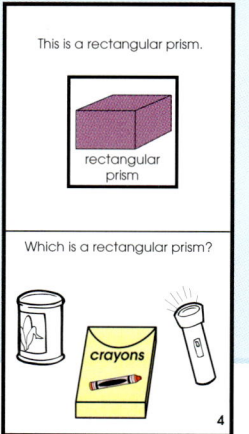
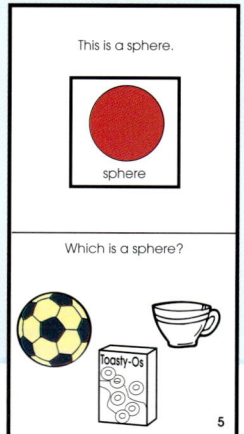

Booklet Cover and Solid Figure Patterns

Cover

Solid Figures

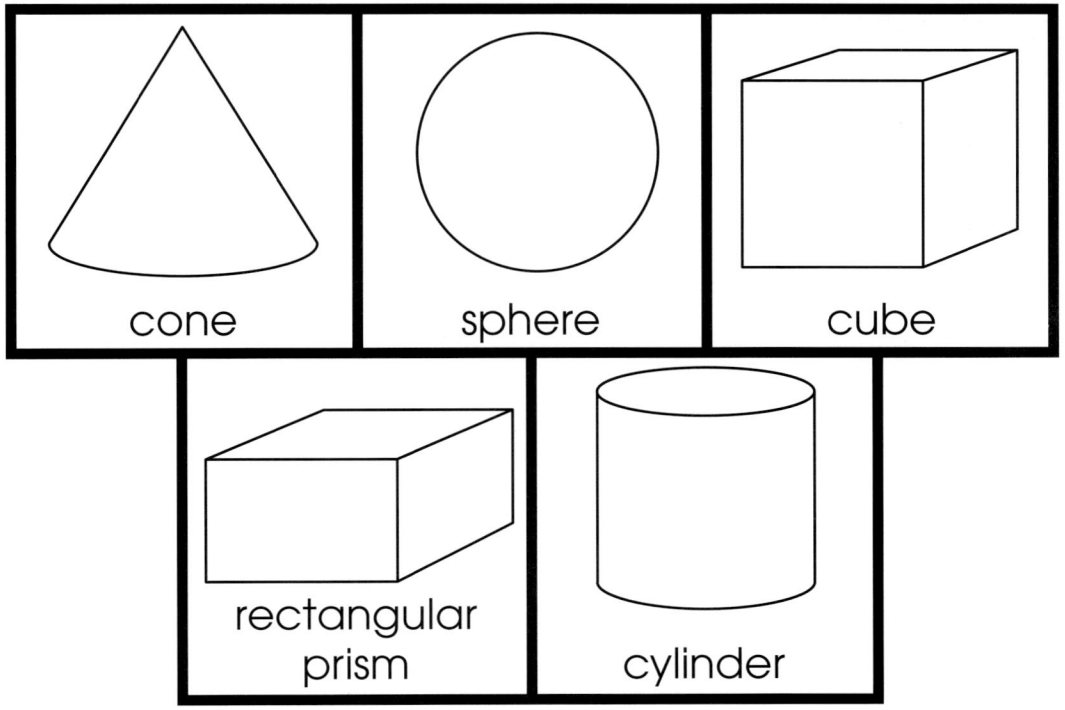

Booklet Page and Sea Lion Pattern

Sea Lion

Booklet Pages

Booklet Pages

This is a rectangular prism.

Which is a rectangular prism?

4

This is a sphere.

Which is a sphere?

5

BEAVER BUILDS A HOUSE

Motivate your youngsters with this enticing shape-review booklet and help Beaver build his house too! Give each student a copy of pages 60–62 and a white sheet of paper. Read the booklet pages with students. Instruct each student to color and cut out the cover. Then have the student cut out the shape patterns and booklet pages along the bold lines. Instruct her to trace a booklet page onto the white sheet of paper and then cut out the tracing. Have the student glue the traced booklet page to the back of booklet page 5 to create a pocket. Next, have the student sequence the pages side by side on her work surface with the cover first. Direct the student to read each page, lay the corresponding shape cutouts on the page, and write the answer(s) in the blank(s). Next, have the student lift the shapes from the page and re-create the featured shape in the corresponding section of the cover. After she completes each page, direct her to place the shape cutouts in the pocket behind page 5. Then tell her to stack the pages in order with the cover on top and staple where indicated. Encourage students to practice reading their booklets with buddies before taking them home to read to their families.

CREATIVE DECORATING OPTION

- As an alternative to the original pocket, glue the back of page 5 in the same manner to the center of a full sheet of green paper. Then decorate the paper to resemble a yard with a swing set or playhouse in the background and flowers in the foreground.

To extend this booklet, have each student draw the outline of a house on a sheet of construction paper. Then give each student a second set of shape patterns (bottom of page 60). Direct the student to cut out the shapes and then glue them to the house to create windows, doors, and a chimney. Instruct the student to write a few sentences about how she made the house.

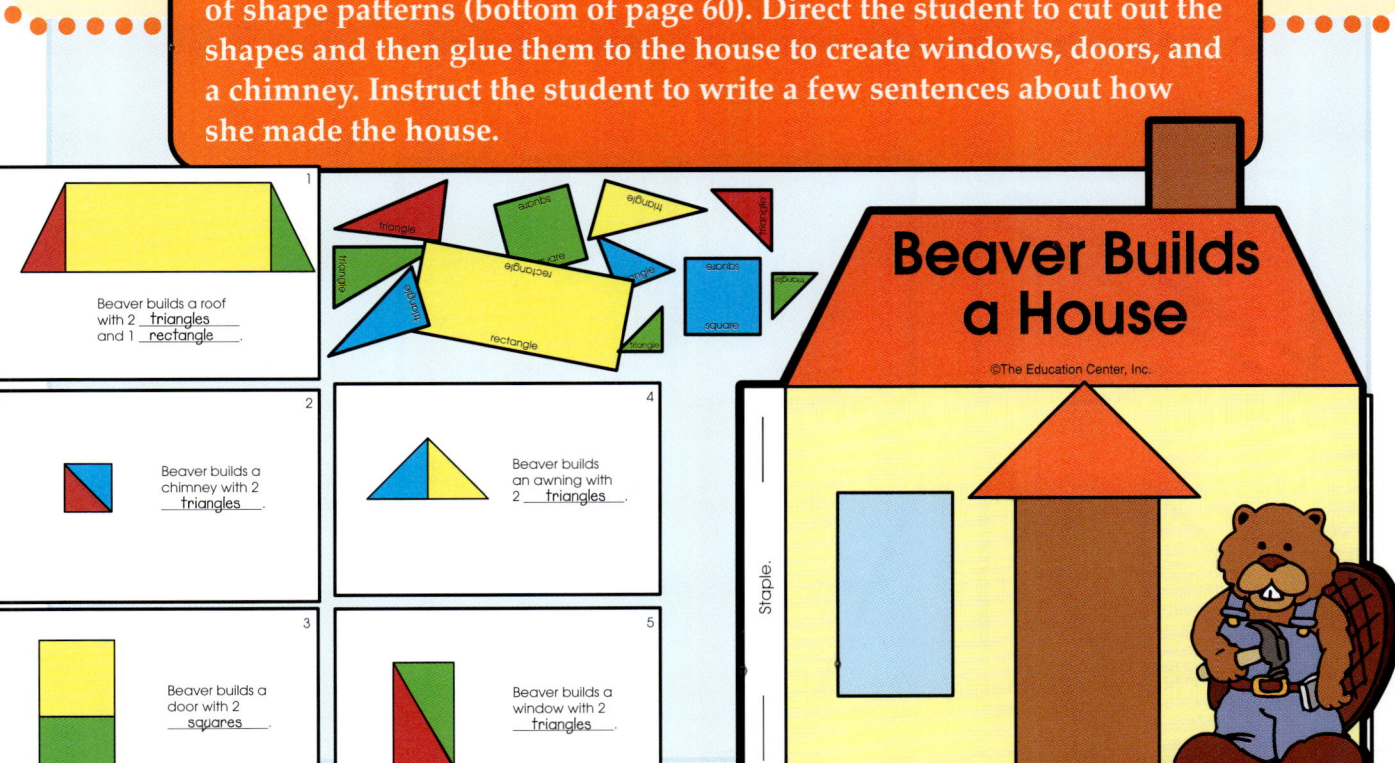

Booklet Cover and Shape Patterns

Cover

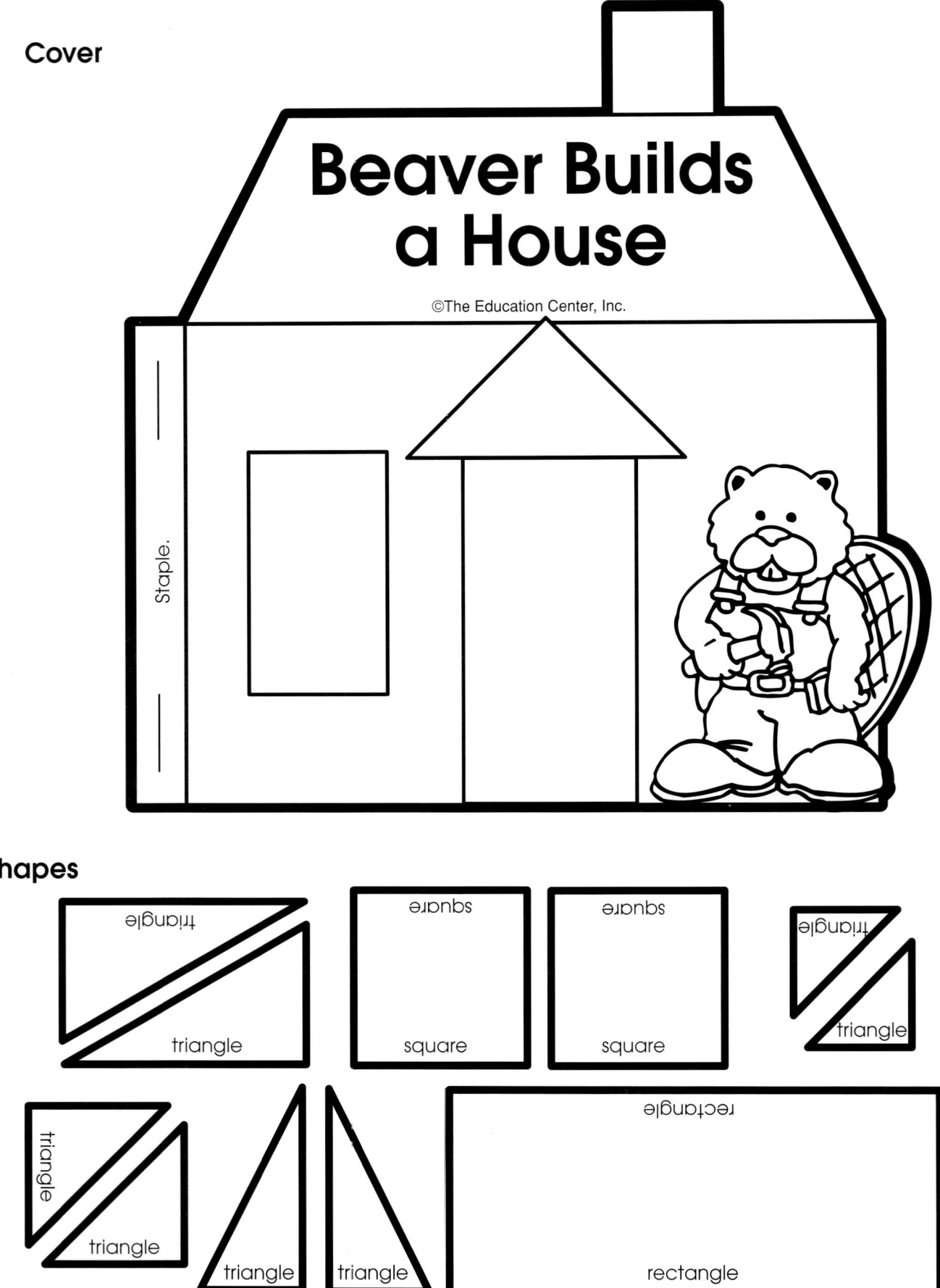

Shapes

©The Education Center, Inc. • *I Can Make It! I Can Read It!* • Math • TEC3520

60 **Note to the teacher:** Use with "Beaver Builds a House" on page 59.

Booklet Pages

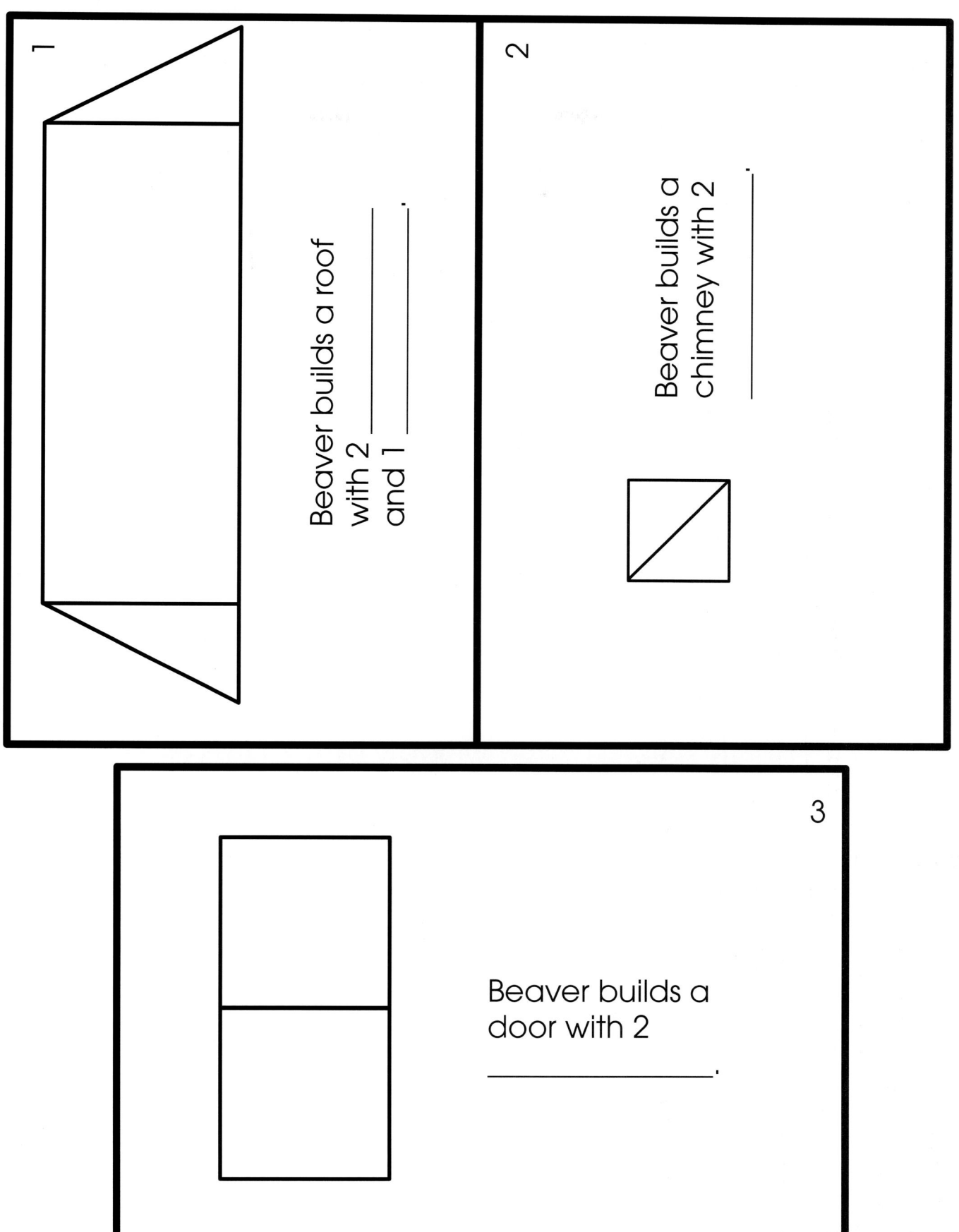

Booklet Pages

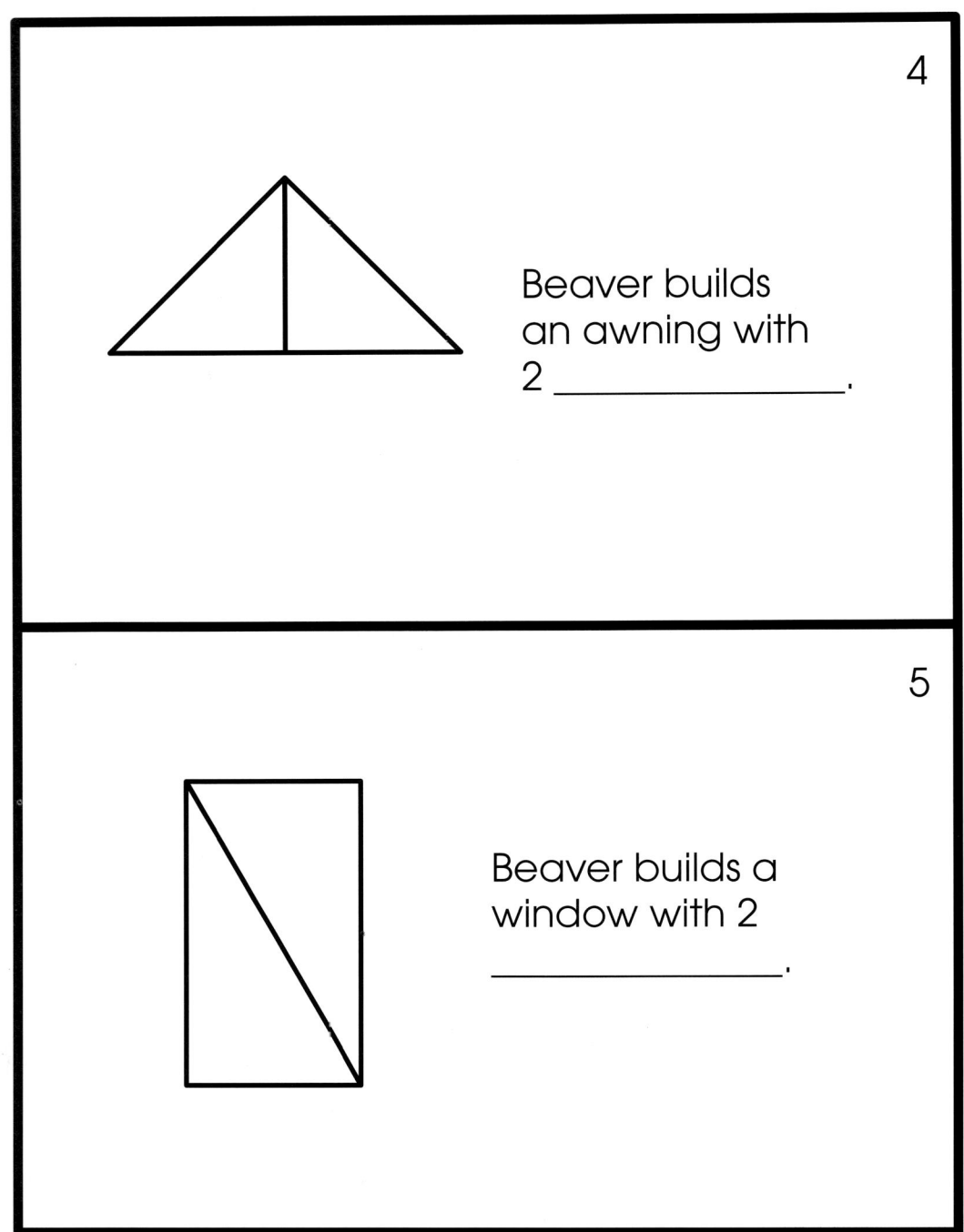

4

Beaver builds an awning with 2 _____.

5

Beaver builds a window with 2 _____.

WORM WAKES UP

Encourage your youngsters to practice their measurement skills with this inviting booklet! Give each student a copy of pages 64–66 and a 6" x 18" strip of construction paper. Read the booklet pages with students. Instruct each student to color and cut out the cover, booklet pages, and worm patterns. (Remind students to color lightly over the text so the booklet can be read.) Have the student arrange the booklet pages in numerical order across the 6" x 18" strip of construction paper and glue them in place as shown. Tell him to trim the excess construction paper off the end of the booklet. Next, help each student accordion-fold his booklet and glue the cover to the front as shown. Then direct him to glue worm pattern A to booklet page 1 where indicated. Have each student read the page, use a ruler to measure the worm from the top of the worm's head to the bottom line where the letter A is shown, and then write the answer in the blank. Have the student repeat this process for worms B, C, and D. Encourage students to practice reading their booklets with buddies before taking them home to read to their families.

CREATIVE DECORATING OPTIONS

- Glue wiggle eyes to the worms.
- Use felt for the worms.

To extend this booklet, change the standard of measurement from inches to centimeters.

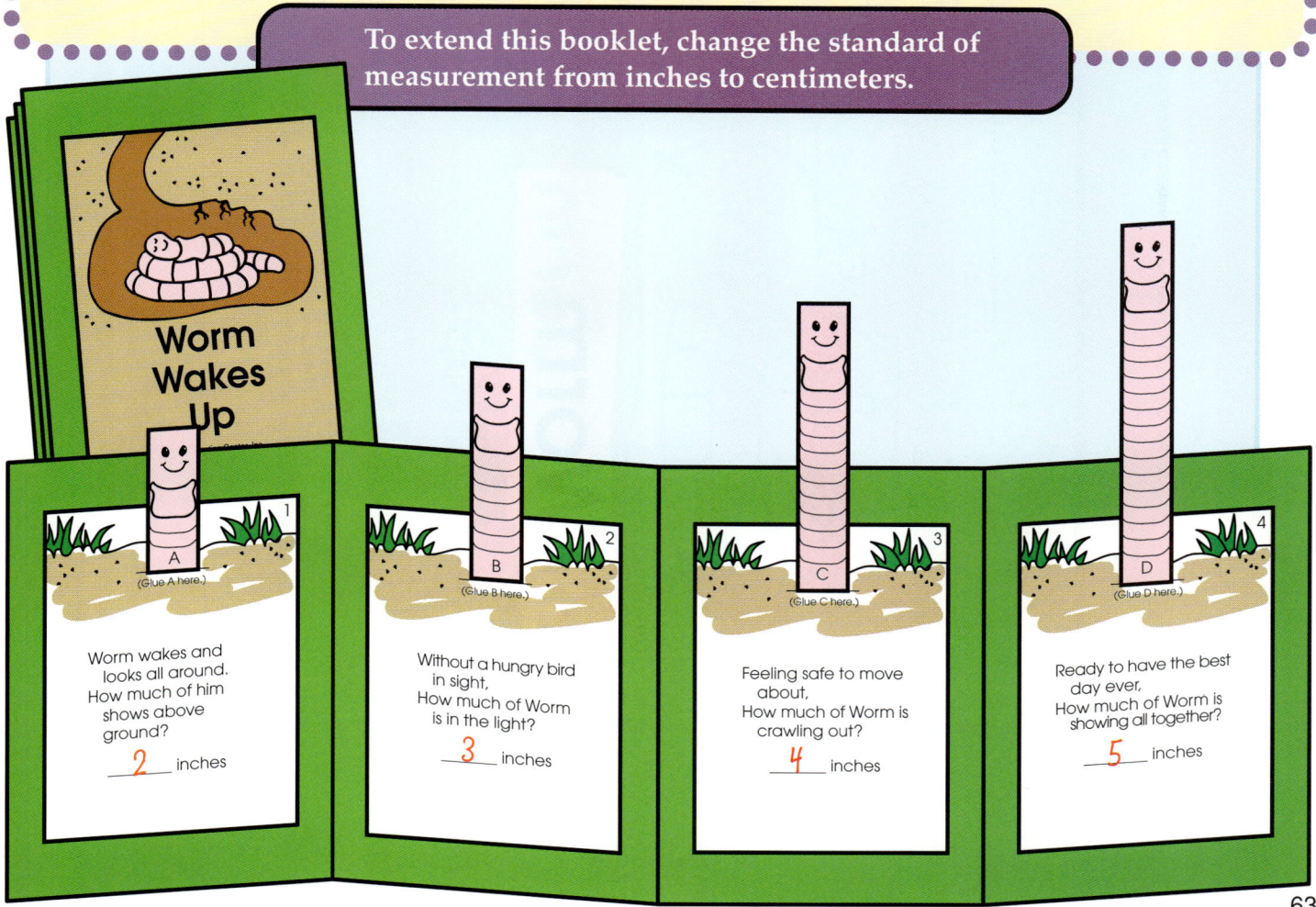

63

Booklet Cover and Page

(Glue A here.)

Worm wakes and looks all around. How much of him shows above ground?

_____ inches

Cover

Inch Worm Wakes Up

3

(Glue C here.)

Feeling safe to move about,
How much of Worm is crawling out?

_____ inches

2

(Glue B here.)

Without a hungry bird in sight,
How much of Worm is in the light?

_____ inches

Booklet Page and Worm Patterns

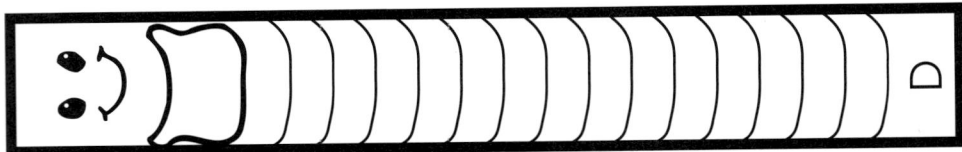

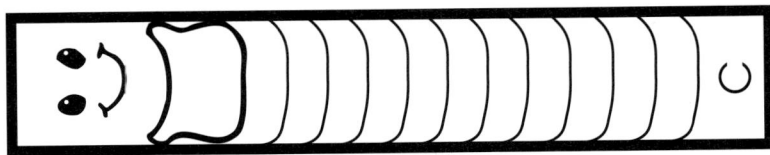

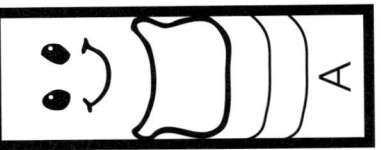

Ready to have the best day ever, How much of Worm is showing all together?

_____ inches

(Glue D here.)

4

Note to the teacher: Use with "Worm Wakes Up" on page 63.

"A-WEIGH" WE GO!

Help your students gain a better understanding of weight as a form of measurement with this interactive booklet. In advance, copy, color, and then cut out the animal pictures on page 71. Then, for each set, tape the heavier animal to a heavier block and the lighter animal to a lighter block. Next, give each child a copy of pages 68–70, one six-inch construction paper square, and one 4" x 6" piece of construction paper. Have each student cut out the title and glue it to the top of the six-inch square to create a backing page. To create a cover, instruct each student to make footprints on the 4" x 6" piece of construction paper using a stamp pad and the side of each fist (for feet) and one finger (for toes) as shown. Tell the student to write her name below the prints. Next, have the student color and cut out booklet pages 1–5. Direct her to glue booklet page 5 below the title on the backing page. Then have the student sequence the booklet pages with the cover on top and the backing page on the bottom. Help her staple the booklet together along the left-hand side.

Store the booklets at a center along with the eight labeled blocks, a balance scale, a class supply of page 71, scissors, crayons, and glue. At the center, direct each student to color and cut out the animal cards from one copy of page 71. Then, for each booklet page 1 through 4, instruct the student to use the scale to measure the corresponding picture blocks. After weighing the blocks, have the student circle the word *more* or *less* to match her findings. Then direct her to glue the corresponding animal cards to the appropriate booklet page. To finish the booklet, have each student complete page 5. After each booklet is complete, have students take their booklets home to read to their families.

CREATIVE DECORATING OPTION

- Use a brad to add a movable hand (like on a clock) to the numbered section on the scale.

To extend this booklet, have pairs of students predict which class objects are heavier, such as a stapler, an eraser, a box of chalk, a pencil, a book, and a backpack. Then have each pair weigh the objects to test the prediction.

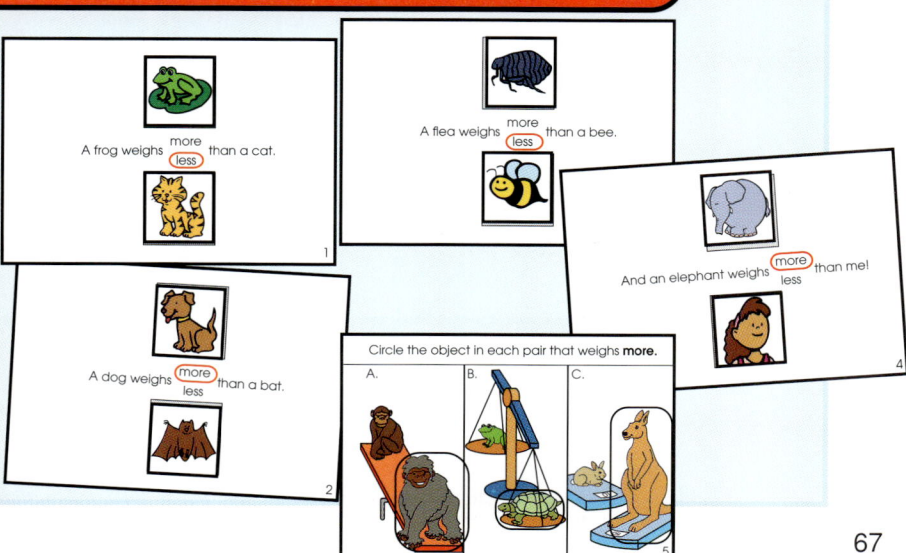

Title Pattern and Booklet Page

Title Pattern

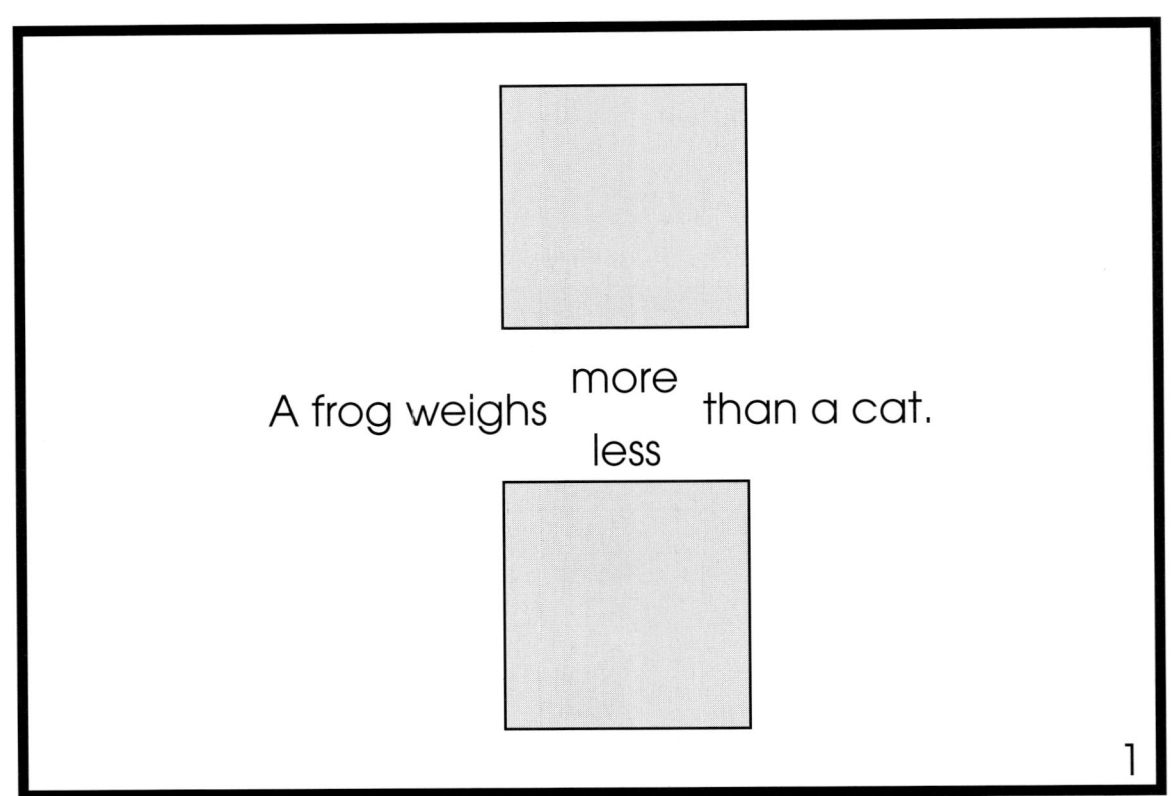

A frog weighs more/less than a cat.

1

Booklet Pages

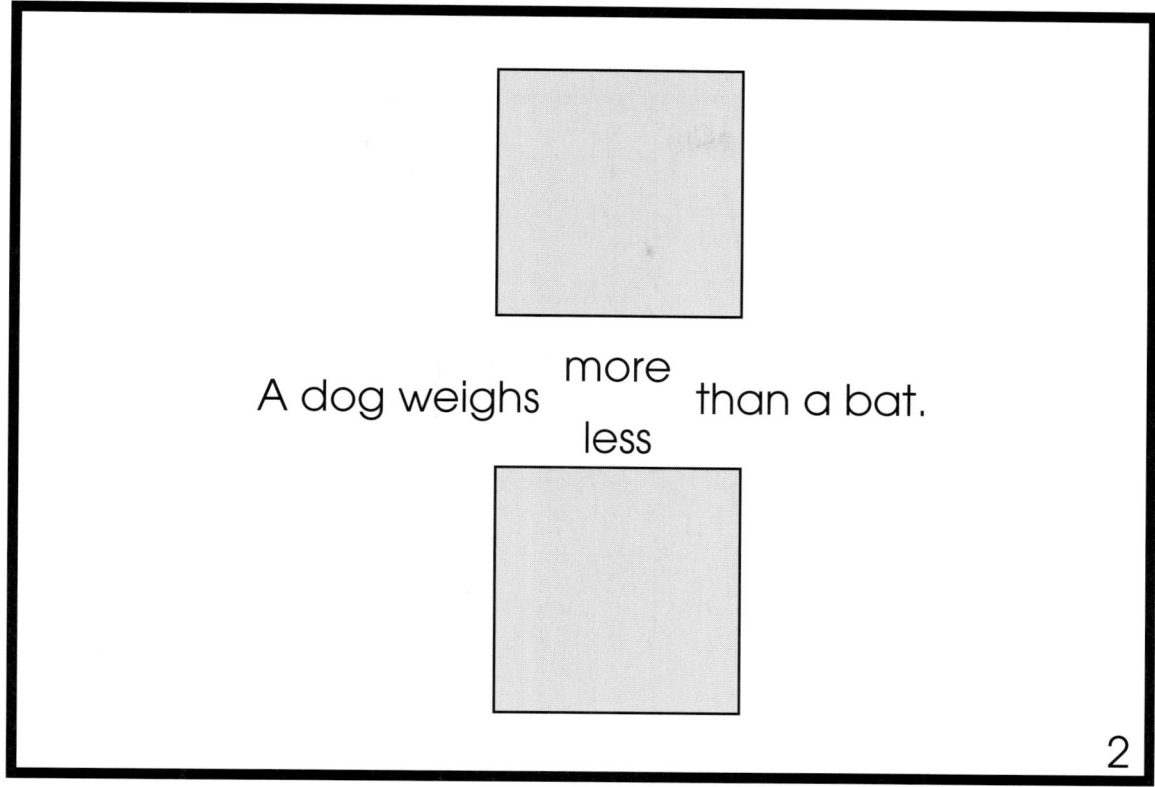

A dog weighs more / less than a bat.

2

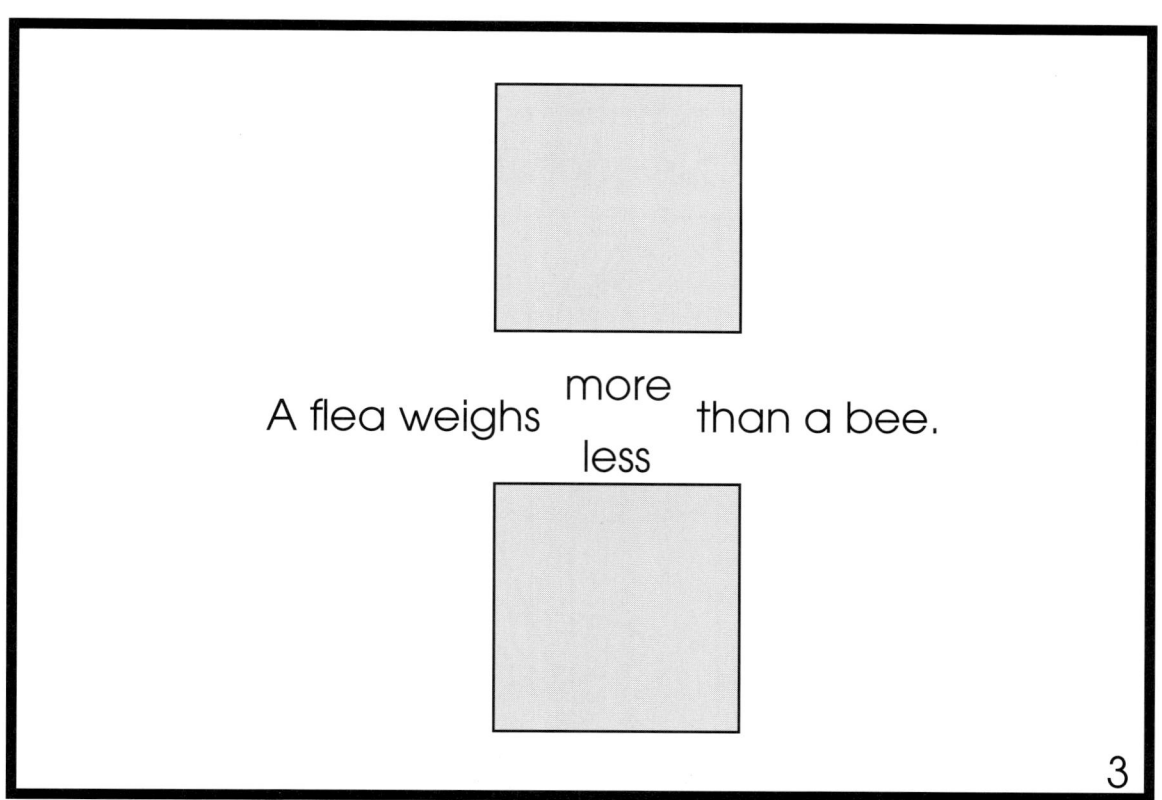

A flea weighs more / less than a bee.

3

Booklet and Backing Pages

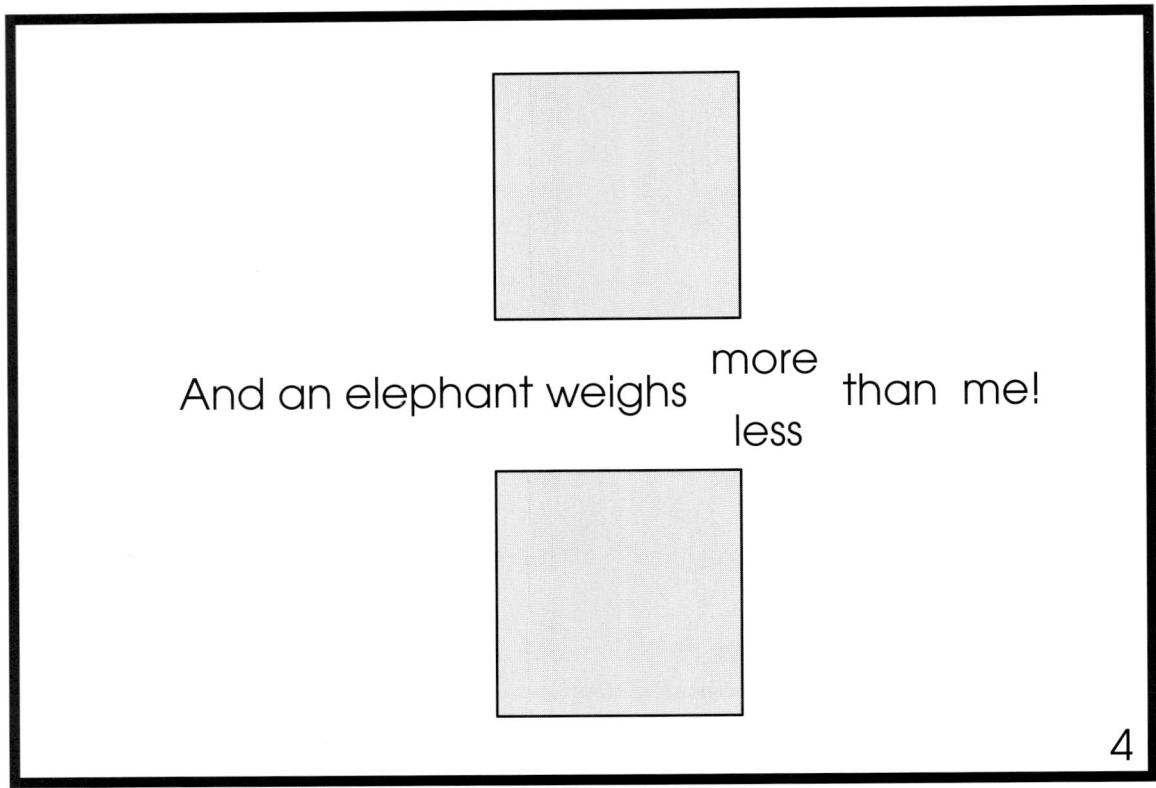

And an elephant weighs more / less than me!

4

Circle the object in each pair that weighs **more**.

A. B. C.

5

Booklet Patterns

Set 1

Set 2

Set 3

Set 4

©The Education Center, Inc. • *I Can Make It! I Can Read It!* • Math • TEC3520

Note to the teacher: Use with " 'A-weigh' We Go!" on page 67.

TICKTOCK!

Telling time has never been more fun than with this barnyard booklet! Duplicate pages 73, 74, and the booklet page and tree pattern on page 75 to make a class supply. Then, for each child, make one white construction paper copy of the rooster and clock pattern on page 75 and the backing page on page 76. Next, give each student two black construction paper clock hands and two brads. Read the booklet pages with students. Instruct each student to color and cut out the cover and the barn door pattern and then glue the back of the right-hand side of the barn door pattern to the right-hand side of the cover where indicated. Instruct the student to color and cut out the rooster and clock pattern, booklet pages, patterns, and backing page. (Remind students to color lightly over the text so the booklet can be read.) Then help him use a brad to attach the clock hands to the clock face where indicated by the X. Next, have the student glue the rooster and clock pattern to the top of the barn where indicated. For booklet pages 1, 3, and 4, tell the student to glue the corresponding patterns as indicated. For page 2, help each student use a brad to attach the hen's head as shown. To assemble the booklet, have each youngster sequence the pages with the cover on top and then staple them to the backing page (page 5) as shown. As each student reads his booklet, have him position the clock hands to represent the time described on each page. Encourage students to practice reading their booklets with buddies before taking them home to read to their families.

CREATIVE DECORATING OPTIONS

- Glue one wiggle eye to Mama Pig on booklet page 1.
- Glue birdseed and yellow pom-poms (chicks) to booklet page 2.
- Glue red sequins (apples) to the tree on booklet page 4.
- Glue straw (hay) to the cover and booklet page 5.

To extend this booklet, adjust the times shown to fit your students' levels. For example, tell time by the quarter hour instead of the half hour.

Cover

Cover, Booklet Page, and Patterns
Barn Door

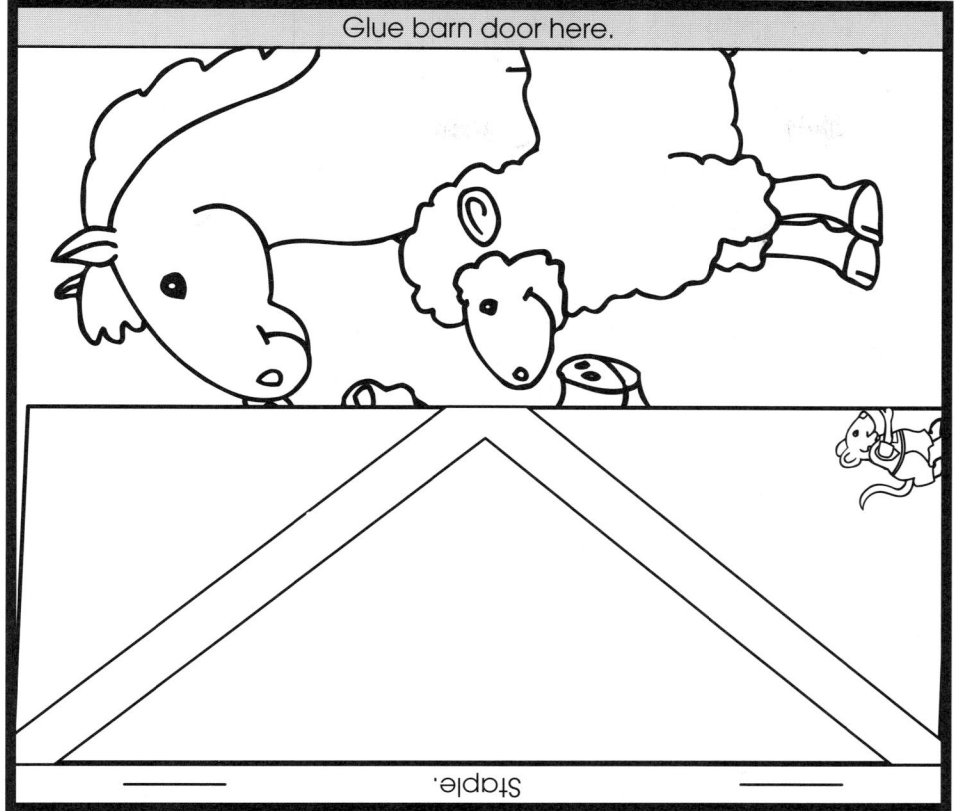

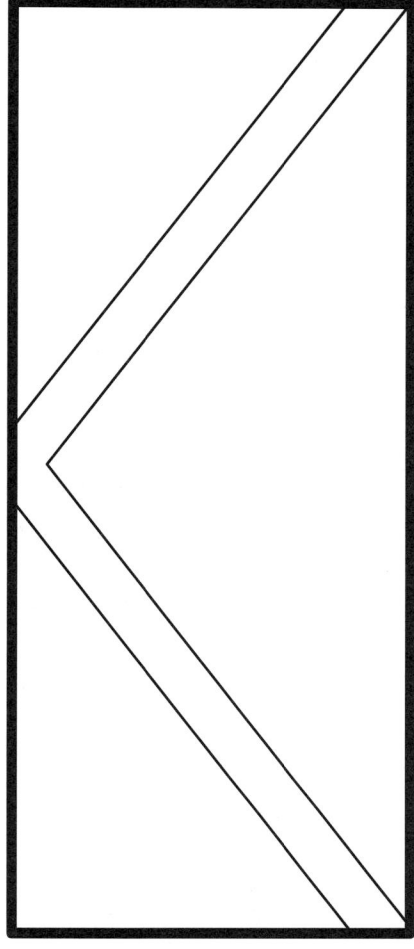

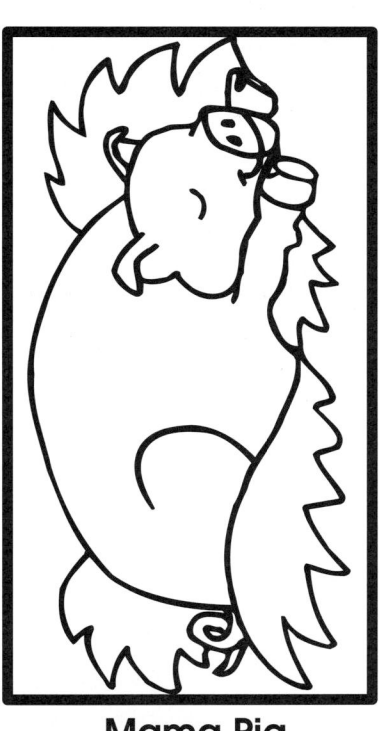

Mama Pig

©The Education Center, Inc. • *I Can Make It! I Can Read It!* • Math • TEC3520

Note to the teacher: Use with "Ticktock!" on page 72.

Booklet Pages and Patterns

At 12:00, the farmer eats lunch and rests under a tree.

3

Picnic Basket

At 9:30, the chickens scratch and peck for seeds.

2

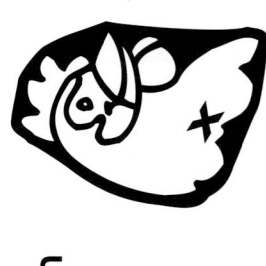

Hen

Booklet Page and Patterns

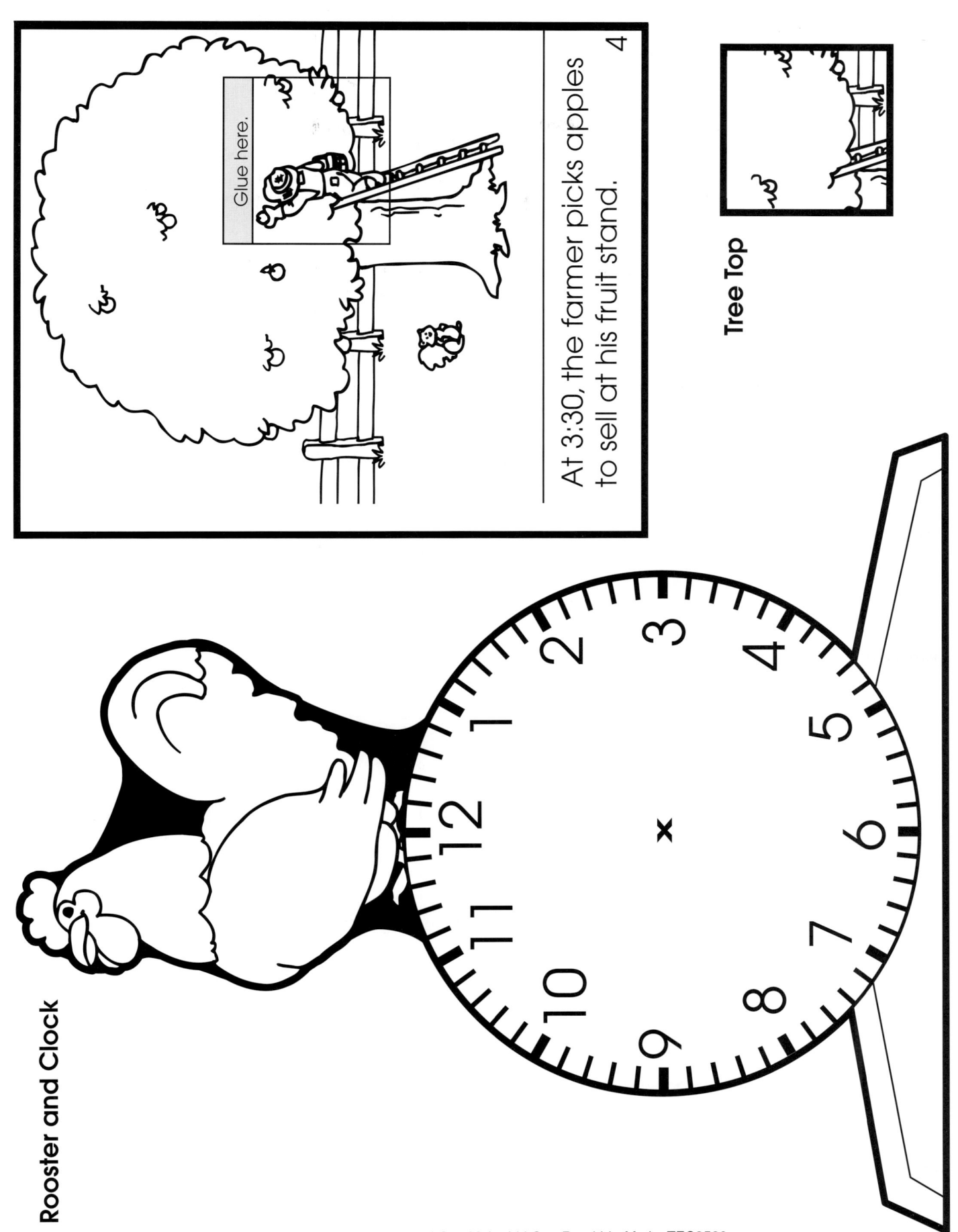

At 3:30, the farmer picks apples to sell at his fruit stand.

Tree Top

Rooster and Clock

Booklet Backing Page

Glue rooster and clock pattern here.

Ticktock!

by _____
Name

Staple.

At 8:30, all is quiet as the animals snuggle in their fresh beds of hay. Good night!

5

©The Education Center, Inc. • *I Can Make It! I Can Read It!* • Math • TEC3520

Note to the teacher: Use with "Ticktock!" on page 72.

A HOME FOR GOLDIE

You're sure to make a splash with students as they explore capacity with this fun booklet-making activity! Give each student a copy of pages 78–81. Instruct the student to color and cut out the cover (page 78) and the patterns (page 81). Then have the student cut out the booklet pages. Direct the student to color the bottoms of booklet pages 1 and 6 brown to represent aquarium gavel. Next, have the student color the top of booklet page 6 blue to represent water. Direct the student to lay her booklet pages in sequential order across her desk. Read the booklet pages with students. Then tell each student to glue the patterns from page 81 to booklet page 6 to match the illustration on the cover. Instruct each student to stack her pages as shown with the cover on top. Help the student staple the pages together. Read page 1 to your students and have them estimate how many gallons it will take to fill Goldie's aquarium. Direct each student to write his estimate in the blank provided. Then show your students that as each page is flipped up, Goldie's aquarium is filled with more water. Be sure to have each student answer the question on page 6. Then have students compare their estimates to the answer. Encourage students to practice reading their booklets with buddies before taking them home to read to their families.

CREATIVE DECORATING OPTION

- Glue colorful aquarium gravel to the bottom of the booklet page 6.

> To extend this booklet, set up a small group center with access to water, a gallon milk jug, paper towels, and a ten-gallon aquarium. As each page is read, let a different student pour into the container the amount of water listed on that booklet page.

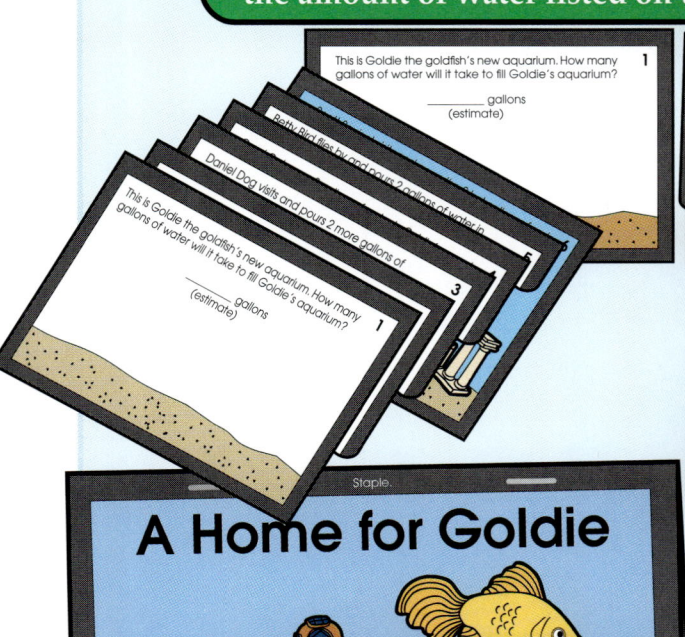

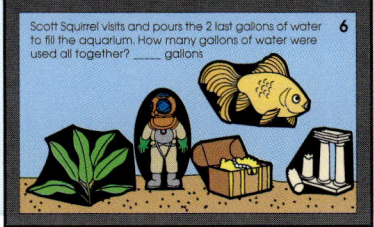

Cover and Booklet Page

A Home for Goldie

Staple.

©The Education Center, Inc. • *I Can Make It! I Can Read It!* • Math • TEC3520

This is Goldie the goldfish's new aquarium. How many gallons of water will it take to fill Goldie's aquarium?

_____ gallons
(estimate)

1

Booklet Page

©The Education Center, Inc. • *I Can Make It! I Can Read It!* • Math • TEC3520

Note to the teacher: Use with "A Home for Goldie" on page 77.

Booklet Pages

2

Max Mouse stops by and pours 2 gallons of water in Goldie's aquarium.

3

Daniel Dog visits and pours 2 more gallons of water in the aquarium.

4

Carol Cat pours 2 gallons of water in Goldie's aquarium.

Betty Bird flies by and pours 2 gallons of water in Goldie's aquarium. **5**

6 Scott Squirrel visits and pours the 2 last gallons of water to fill the aquarium. How many gallons of water were used all together? _____ gallons

 Note to the teacher: Use with "A Home for Goldie" on page 77.

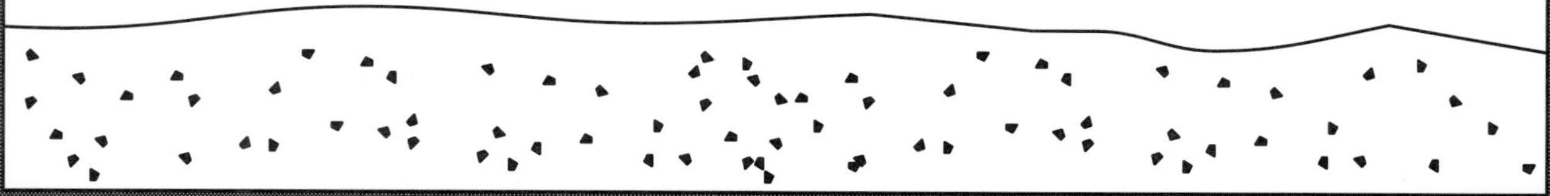

Booklet Patterns

Castle

Diver

Goldie

Treasure Chest

Plant

©The Education Center, Inc. • *I Can Make It! I Can Read It!* • Math • TEC3520

Note to the teacher: Use with "A Home for Goldie" on page 77.

WHICH MOUSE MEASURES UP?

Entice your students to practice their measuring skills with this "mice-y" good booklet activity! In advance, gather a class supply of rulers as well as a variety of nonstandard measurement devices, such as small paper clips, lengths of yarn, and Unifix cubes. Give each youngster a copy of pages 83–86, a pencil, crayons, scissors, and glue. Read the booklet pages with students. Instruct each student to color and cut out the cover, booklet pages, and patterns. (Remind students to color lightly over the text so the booklet can be read.) For each page, tell each student to use a different measuring device to determine the answer to the question, glue a ribbon from page 83 to the corresponding mouse, and write the mouse's name in the space provided. Instruct each student to stack her pages in numerical order with the cover on top. Help the student staple the pages together along the top. Encourage students to practice reading their booklets with buddies before taking them home to read to their families.

CREATIVE DECORATING OPTIONS

- Place a decorative sticker ribbon on the booklet cover.
- Glue lengths of black yarn over the whiskers on the cover.

To extend this booklet, divide the class into pairs or small groups. Give each group a piece of poster board. Instruct the group to draw a mouse with the measurements you name (for example, a mouse that is two feet tall, has a tail that is 40 inches long, and whiskers that are five inches long). Display the completed works on a bulletin board titled "Mouse-Sized Measurements."

Which mouse has the longest tail? **Miffy** 1

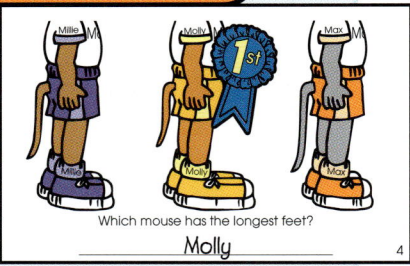

Which mouse has the longest feet? **Molly** 4

Which mouse has the longest whiskers? **Max** 2

Which mouse is the tallest? **Millie** 5

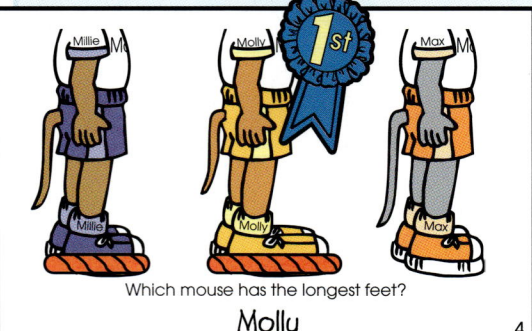

Which mouse has the longest feet? **Molly** 4

Which mouse has the longest arms? **Marty** 3

We are **all** great! 6

Cover

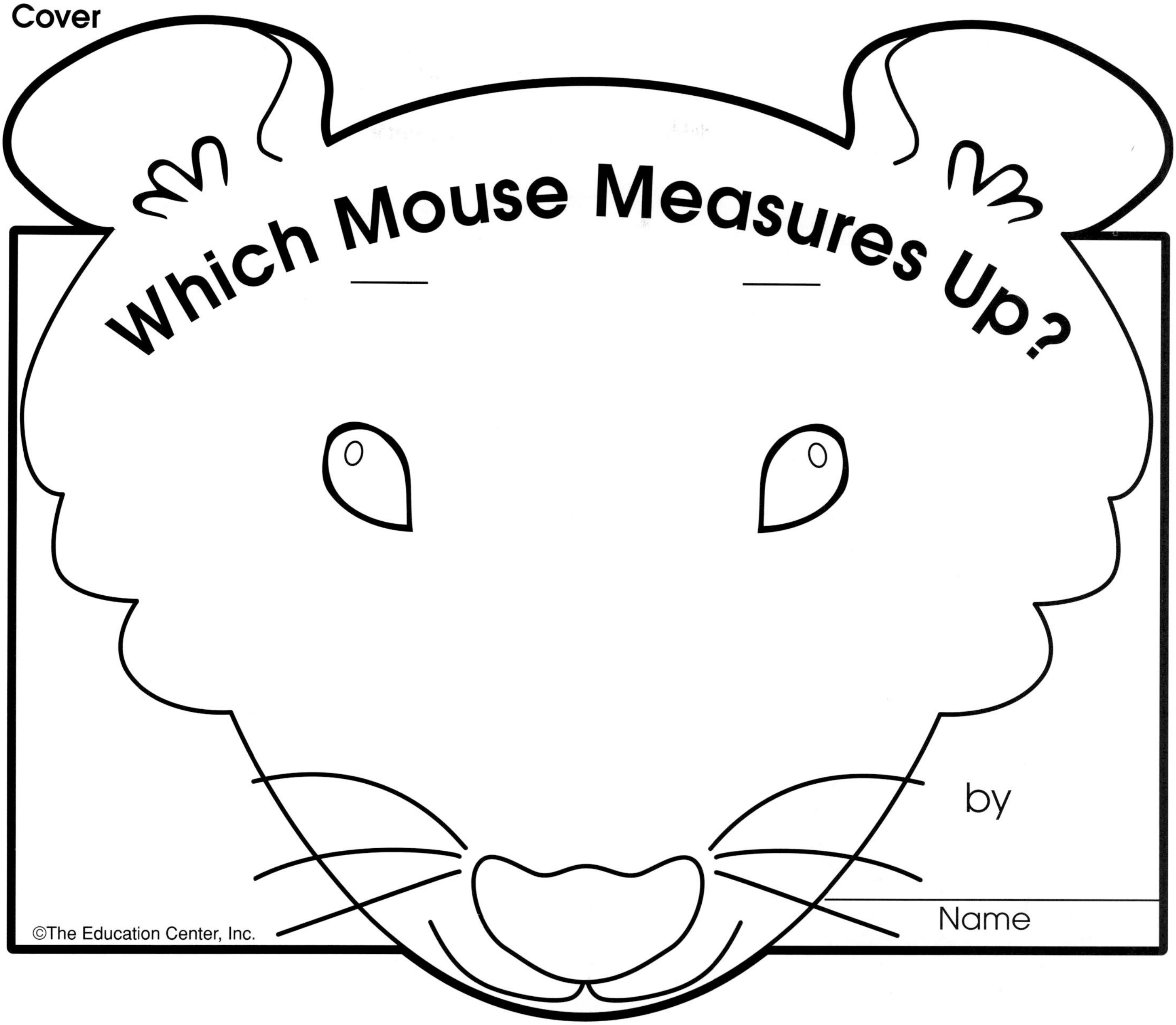

Booklet Cover and Patterns

Which Mouse Measures Up?

by

Name

©The Education Center, Inc.

Ribbons

©The Education Center, Inc. • *I Can Make It! I Can Read It!* • Math • TEC3520

Note to the teacher: Use with "Which Mouse Measures Up?" on page 82.

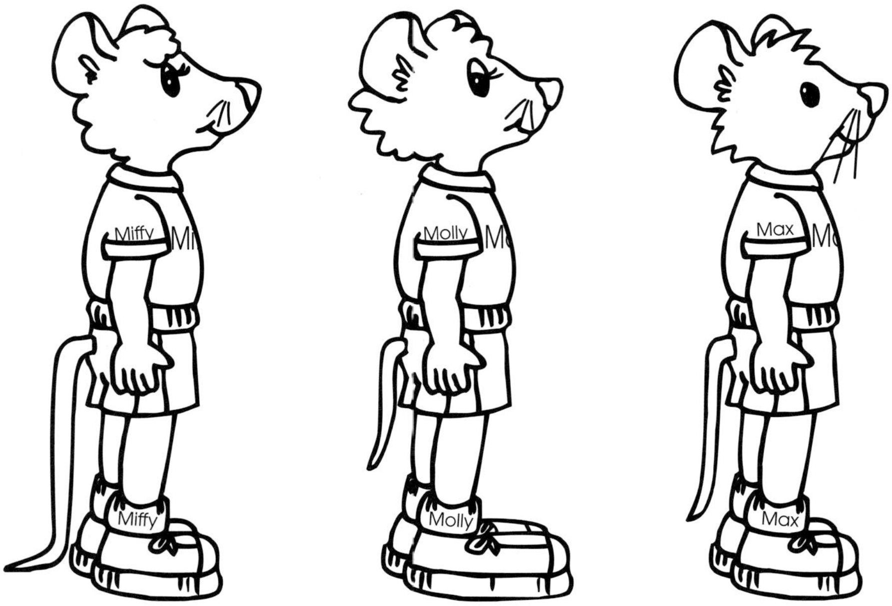

Booklet Pages

Which mouse has the longest tail?

_____ 1

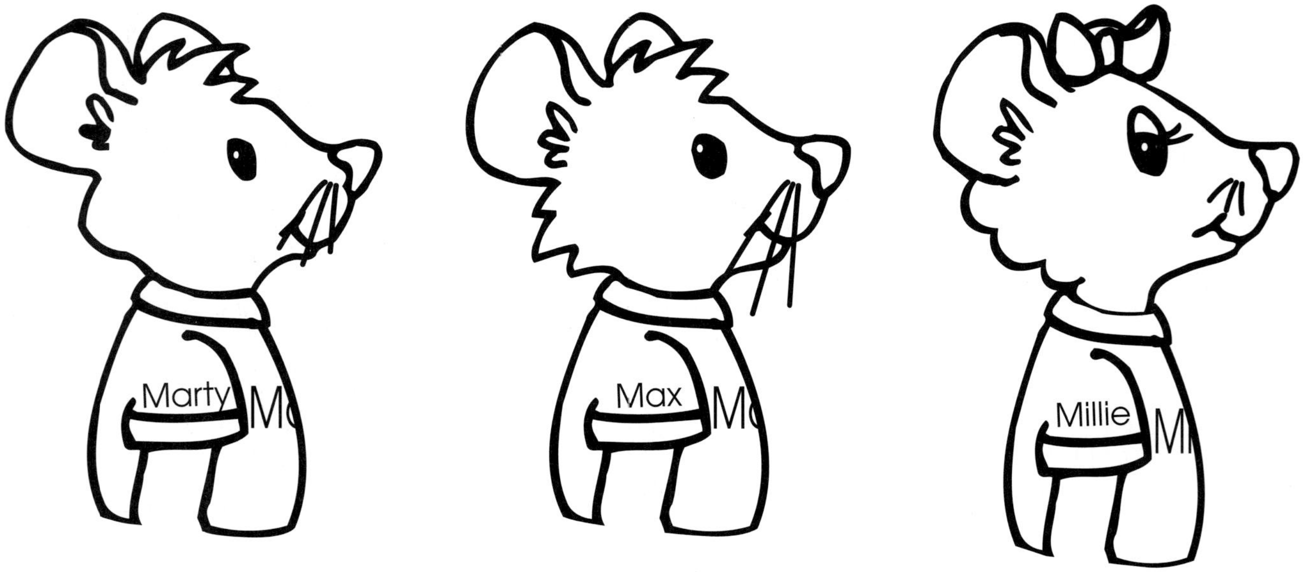

Which mouse has the longest whiskers?

_____ 2

Booklet Pages

Which mouse has the longest arms?

3

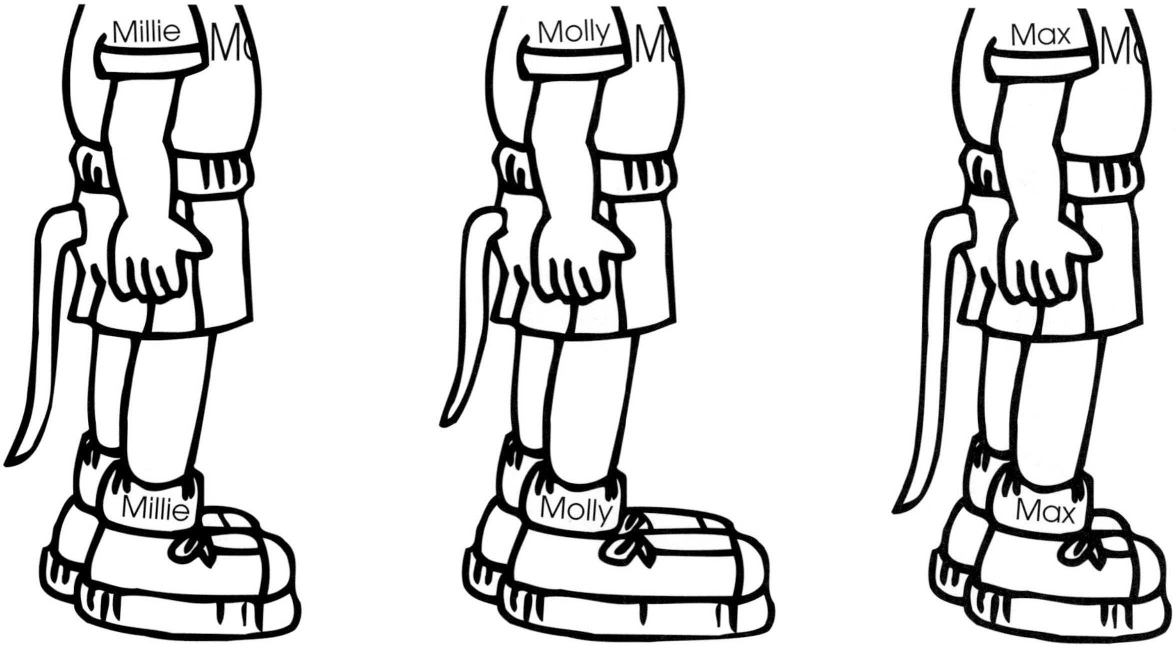

Which mouse has the longest feet?

4

©The Education Center, Inc. • *I Can Make It! I Can Read It!* • Math • TEC3520

Note to the teacher: Use with "Which Mouse Measures Up?" on page 82.

Booklet Pages

Which mouse is the tallest?

_____

5

We are **all** great!

6

©The Education Center, Inc. • *I Can Make It! I Can Read It!* • Math • TEC3520

86　**Note to the teacher:** Use with "Which Mouse Measures Up?" on page 82.

GRAPHING GARDEN GOODIES

Plant the seeds of graphing knowledge with this booklet of garden goodies! Give each student a copy of pages 88–91. Read the booklet pages with students. Then instruct each student to color his cover, counters, and booklet pages and cut them out along the bold lines. (Remind students to color lightly over the text so the page can be read.) To complete the booklet, have each youngster read each page and then glue the corresponding number of counters to the graph on the cover. After completing the graph, instruct the student to use its information to complete booklet page 6. Next, direct the student to glue the pages together where indicated. Once the glue has dried, help him accordion-fold the booklet. Invite each student to read his completed booklet with a partner before taking it home to share with family members.

CREATIVE DECORATING OPTIONS

- Use colored chalk to color each page.
- For alternative counters, use the corresponding dried seeds to represent each food item listed in the graph.

To extend this booklet activity, invite each student to select which garden goodie is his favorite. Instruct him to draw a picture of the food and then write a descriptive sentence about it.

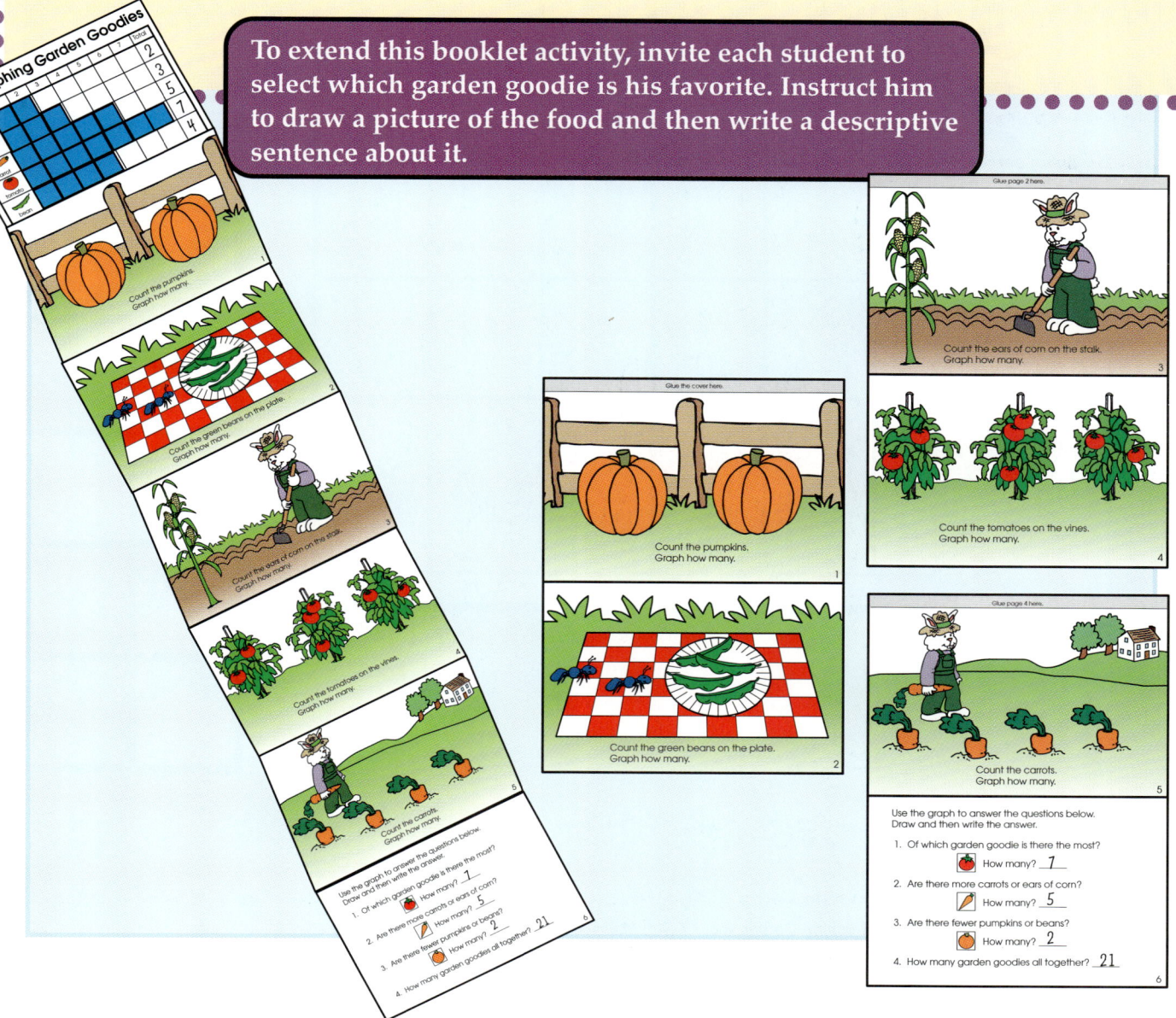

Booklet Cover and Counters

Cover

Graphing Garden Goodies

	1	2	3	4	5	6	7	Total
pumpkin								
corn								
carrot								
tomato								
bean								

Counters

Note to the teacher: Use with "Graphing Garden Goodies" on page 87.

Booklet Pages

Glue page 2 here.

Count the ears of corn on the stalk.
Graph how many.

3

Count the tomatoes on the vines.
Graph how many.

4

©The Education Center, Inc. • *I Can Make It! I Can Read It!* • Math • TEC3520

Booklet Pages

Glue page 4 here.

Count the carrots.
Graph how many.

5

Use the graph to answer the questions below.
Draw and then write the answer.

1. Of which garden goodie is there the most?
   ☐ How many? _____

2. Are there more carrots or ears of corn?
   ☐ How many? _____

3. Are there fewer pumpkins or beans?
   ☐ How many? _____

4. How many garden goodies all together? _____

6

©The Education Center, Inc. • *I Can Make It! I Can Read It!* • Math • TEC3520

Note to the teacher: Use with "Graphing Garden Goodies" on page 87.

HOW MANY ANIMALS ARE IN THE ZOO?

Use this pictograph booklet to make counting zoo animals a cinch! Give each student a copy of pages 93–96. Read the booklet pages with students. Then instruct each student to color her cover and booklet pages and cut them out along the bold lines. (Remind students to color lightly over the text so the pages can be read.) Then have each student cut the cover and booklet pages apart along the dotted lines. Next, help her sequence and stack the pages in two sets with the cover pages on top; then staple each set of pages to the backing page as shown. To complete the booklet, have the student read each left-hand page, count the featured animal on the pictograph located on the backing page, and then write the corresponding number in the blank box on the right-hand page. After completing each set of pages, instruct the student to read her completed booklet with a partner before taking it home to share with family members.

CREATIVE DECORATING OPTION

- Use tempera paint to decorate each page.

To extend this booklet activity, reread the booklet and invite the appropriate number of students to role-play the animal featured on each page.

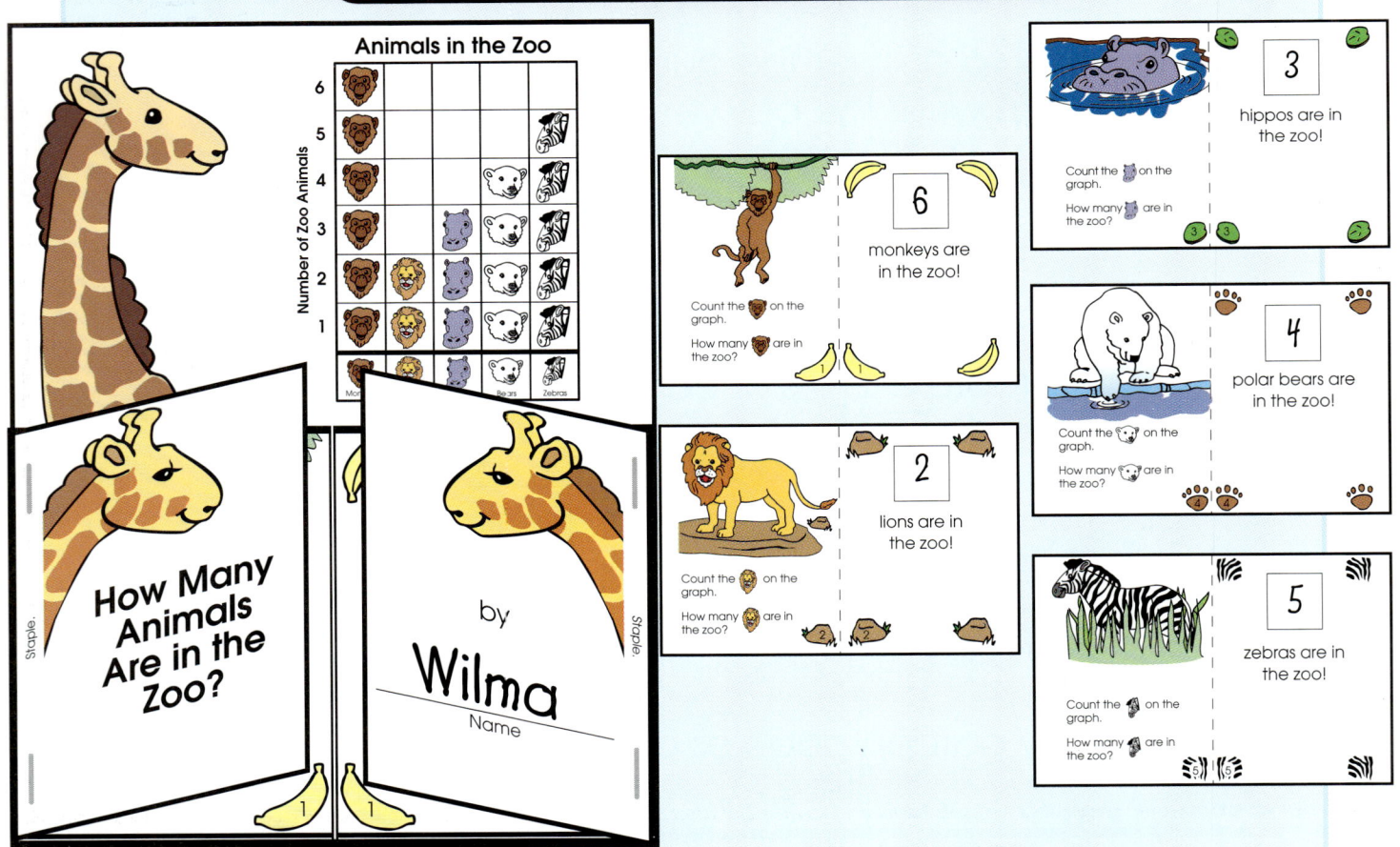

Cover and Booklet Pages

Staple.

How Many Animals Are in the Zoo?

by

_____
Name

Staple.

©The Education Center, Inc.

_____ monkeys are in the zoo!

Count the 🐵 on the graph.

How many 🐵 are in the zoo?

©The Education Center, Inc. • *I Can Make It! I Can Read It!* • Math • TEC3520

Note to the teacher: Use with "How Many Animals Are in the Zoo?" on page 92.

Booklet Pages

polar bears are in the zoo!

Count the  on the graph.

How many  are in the zoo?

zebras are in the zoo!

Count the on the graph.

How many are in the zoo?

©The Education Center, Inc. • *I Can Make It! I Can Read It!* • Math • TEC3520